A Canadian Nurse in the Great War

The Diaries of Ruth Loggie, 1915–1916

Edited by ROSS HEBB

NIMBUS PUBLISHING
NIMBUS.CA

Nimbus Publishing Limited
3660 Strawberry Hill Street, Halifax, NS, B3K 5A9
(902) 455-4286 nimbus.ca

Printed and bound in Canada

NB1539

Editor: Marianne Ward
Cover design: Heather Bryan
Interior Design: Jenn Embree
All images generously provided by John Gass (nephew of Clare Gass)

Library and Archives Canada Cataloguing in Publication

Title: A Canadian nurse in the Great War : the diaries of Ruth Loggie, 1915-1916 / edited by Ross Hebb.
Other titles: Diaries of Ruth Loggie, 1915-1916
Names: Loggie, Ruth, author. | Hebb, Ross N., 1960- editor.
Identifiers: Canadiana 20210215410 | ISBN 9781774710128 (softcover)
Subjects: LCSH: Loggie, Ruth—Diaries. | LCSH: Nurses—Canada—Diaries. | LCSH: World War, 1914-1918—Personal narratives, Canadian. | LCSH: World War, 1914-1918—Medical care—Canada. | LCSH: World War, 1914-1918—Women—Canada. | LCGFT: Diaries.
Classification: LCC D630.L64 A3 2021 | DDC 940.4/7571—dc23

Canada

Canada Council for the Arts | Conseil des arts du Canada

NOVA SCOTIA

Nimbus Publishing acknowledges the financial support for its publishing activities from the Government of Canada, the Canada Council for the Arts, and from the Province of Nova Scotia. We are pleased to work in partnership with the Province of Nova Scotia to develop and promote our creative industries for the benefit of all Nova Scotians.

FSC www.fsc.org MIX Paper from responsible sources FSC® C013916

Dedicated to the memory of the Great War nurses of the Canadian Army Medical Corps and to the McGill graduate I love and admire, my wife, Linda M. Hebb, MD, CM; CCFP (EM); FCFP.

Contents

Acknowledgements

A WORK SUCH AS THIS IS A COLLABORATIVE EFFORT spanning several years. First, I would like to thank Ron Stevenson for initially bringing to my attention the existence of Ruth's wartime diaries. Next, Barbara Wilson's enthusiasm and willingness to share the manuscript text as well as her knowledge of Ruth provided watershed moments in the journey. I also wish to thank the Historical Committee of the Burnt Church and New Jersey Senior Citizens Group for the opportunity to examine Ruth's 1916 diary. On two separate occasions Margaret McLeod welcomed me to their facility. Dedicated volunteer local groups such as theirs are a key factor in finding, preserving, and perpetuating our history. As always, the staff at the Provincial Archives of New Brunswick extended to me every courtesy and professional assistance in examining the 1915 diary. John Gass, Clare Gass's nephew and the keeper of her valuable wartime photo album, was both generous and most patient in providing scans of precious photographs even under COVID-19 pandemic restrictions. I would be remiss not to note the assistance of my initial proofreader, Wilfred Alliston. For the past twenty-five years he has not only helped improve my writing, but has also come to intuit what I am attempting to communicate. Nimbus editor Marianne Ward also has a keen eye for detail and required me to explain myself, which doubtless has served to improve the final copy.

Introduction

THE GREAT WAR DIARIES OF RUTH LOGGIE ARE A RARE find.[1] Their pages grant us a unique peek into a little-known moment of our history. They are indeed rare, for while 420,000 men served overseas during the Great War, only 2,100 Canadian women served as army nurses.[2] To be able to read a diary of one of these women, a document that was, strictly speaking, not supposed to be kept in the first place, is a great privilege. Not only are diaries and letters of Canadian Great War nurses scarce,[3] but they are special in other ways as well. They provide a glimpse into a part of our history that up to that point had been forbidden territory—women at war.

Canadian nurses were part of the Canadian Expeditionary Force (CEF) and actively involved in our country's war effort. They were part of the Canadian Army Medical Corps (CAMC), whose task it was to care for wounded soldiers. What that meant was, if at all possible, to heal the soldier, not so that he could come home, but so that he could rejoin the fight. Although shielded from actual combat, Canadian nurses did serve in France and Belgium. While initially kept back from the front, nurses did eventually function in forward areas known as Casualty Clearing Stations (CCS) well within the range of enemy artillery fire. In addition, by 1918, the extensive system of tent hospitals at the French coast where most of the nurses were stationed became subject to almost nightly attack by enemy bombers. In sum, by war's end, being a nurse on the continent was not only dangerous but deadly. As a result, Canadian nurses, like the men they cared for, lie buried in French soil.

Not only are the stories of Great War nurses little known, but there is also a distinct paucity of their experiences in the historical record. The official history of Canada's medical services in the Great War only contains six pages, written by Matron MacDonald, on the contribution of nurses during the war.[4] Amazingly, there was no attempt to write an actual history of their participation and service until *Canada's Nursing Sisters* by G. W. L. Nicholson appeared in 1975. Regrettably, this survey work attempted to cover all Canadian nursing history up to that time and devoted a mere fifty pages to the Great War. In was not until 2016, a full century after the war, that Cynthia Toman's *Sister Soldiers of the Great War: The Nurses of the Canadian Army Medical Corps* appeared. This extraordinary gap in our nation's historical record is not simply attributable to male bias and prevailing societal attitudes. The nurses themselves contributed to the lack of a record of their collective experience. When an immediate postwar attempt was made to record their contribution and experience, the nurses failed to respond to the request for details and personal experiences. Tellingly, this lack of recording of Great War nursing experience is not a uniquely Canadian predicament. A similar trajectory of silence and piecemeal historical research has characterized the British experience as well.[5]

Why Canadian nurses almost universally neglected to respond to the request from their own leader for source material has, in recent decades, baffled historians and women's studies professors. A plausible answer seems to lie in the combined effect of three interconnected considerations.

First, in the immediate postwar period, when the first request for information was made, the majority of nurses had other more pressing matters to attend to: reintegration into civilian society and employment. With as much as four years of military nursing overseas and a depressed postwar job market, Canada's returned military nurses had little time to pause and reflect. They had to settle down, find employment, and get on with their lives. Second, each nurse was hard-pressed to see her particular experience as worthy of note. All the other nurses she encountered had had similar experiences, and she considered that she had just "done her bit." Furthermore, compared to those of the "boys" these women nursed, their experiences seemed, to the nurses themselves, light and of little interest. Reinforcing this reality, the Canadian public and the press on the "home front" had for years been obsessed with battles and bravery, not nurses and wounds. Third, and perhaps most telling, the very nature of the nursing profession, which they epitomized, taught them to be self-effacing, humble, and to keep confidences. Chattering about the men they nursed and the experiences they had had was exactly what they were taught not to do. The nurses had internalized this message, and they clearly endorsed its emphasis on discretion and quiet. A further proof of this collective reticence is the fact that only four of the Canadian nurses individually and independently published any account of their personal experiences during the remainder of their lives (see note 3).

Notwithstanding these sentiments, there is another component to Great War nurses' service that is seldom given sufficient weight in the historical narrative: what these nurses actually saw and worked with on a regular basis, the reality of modern, industrialized warfare. In short, they witnessed firsthand the application of recent advances in modern science to the business of killing other humans. Just like the soldiers in

Ruth Loggie enjoying a relaxed moment in her living quarters, Boulogne, July 18, 1916.

the trenches, the nurses saw the gaping shrapnel wounds, the gas victims gasping for oxygen, and the steady stream of pitiful, mangled men. As Ruth commented early in her experience, "All our men are splendid [patients] and some so badly cut up."[6] Along with the doctors and orderlies, this was the nurses' wartime environment. It was what they lived in and worked with—in many cases, including Ruth Loggie's—for four years. How did they cope? What were their thoughts as they lived through what they knew were world-altering events?

Ruth Loggie's diary gives us a daily commentary on her life as she experienced it and as the events of the Great War unfolded. Raw, fresh, unedited, and immediate, it is a special document, but it requires context. Ruth was but one nurse of hundreds in the CAMC, working in one of many Canadian hospitals in France as part of the Canadian contribution to the British Empire's war effort. We need to place her experience within the broader context.

THE OUTBREAK OF WAR AND THE CAMC

When the British Empire went to war in August 1914, so too did Canada. When the British Government initially asked Canada to raise a contingent of 25,000 men, the Dominion responded enthusiastically. The First Contingent, which sailed in early October 1914, was actually 33,000 strong and included 105 nurses.[7] As with the men who initially volunteered in numbers well beyond those required, so too many more nurses applied than were needed. Canadian Matron in Charge, Margaret MacDonald of Nova Scotia, carefully selected the "right sort of women" from the available pool of applicants. The basic requirements included: being a British subject; being between the ages of twenty-one and thirty-eight at the time of enlistment; physical fitness; being of high moral character, unmarried,[8] and a graduate nurse. Of all the listed criteria, the last was the essential one. A nurse had to be a graduate of a recognized hospital training program. This criteria explicitly excluded the slightly skilled enthusiasts known as VADs (Voluntary Aid Detachment women) that were so common in British hospitals. The recognized three-year nurse training programs guaranteed the required level of knowledge, skills, discipline, obedience, endurance, and moral character. The hospital training schools, either in Canada or the United States, were run in such a manner as to imbue their graduates with military-style discipline and obedience. Furthermore, the training schools, along with the nascent graduate nursing associations, had been advocating for "professional status and legal recognition since the early 1900s."[9] Matron MacDonald was wholly in step with the drive for professionalization and recognition and insisted that all nurses admitted to the CAMC be graduate nurses.

While Ruth Loggie was not among the First Contingent nurses of 1914, she did apply to the CAMC in the spring of 1915. Her attestation file reveals that she was born in the little fishing village of Burnt Church, New Brunswick, on July 18, 1883, making her thirty-one at the time of her enlistment. It further confirms that she was an unmarried graduate nurse, standing five feet six inches tall with dark hair and blue eyes. Ruth's Burnt Church family ran a general store and had business interests in supplying the local fishing industry.[10] While her four unmarried brothers and two sisters helped run the family business, Ruth was able to pursue other interests. Having secured an education beyond the elementary, at age twenty-four Ruth was able to move to the biggest city of the Dominion and secure a nursing degree, graduating from Montreal General Hospital in 1910.[11]

Before the outbreak of hostilities, Canada's military medical services had been bare bones. Indeed, there were only five nurses in the permanent force prior to 1914. What was in place, however, was unique. Unlike all other Allied military forces, including the British, Canadian nurses were actually part of the army. Nurses had been granted officer rank (lieutenant), distinct and visually striking dress uniforms, and a pay scale commensurate with the rank given.[12] However, with the rank and pay came the military's control of their nurses. Unlike other nations who essentially outsourced nursing services to the Red Cross or the Queen Alexander Imperial Military Nursing Service (QAIMNS), Canadian nurses were part of the army. Although justly famous as the founder of modern nursing, Florence Nightingale was remembered within certain military circles for her unrelenting criticism of the British Army's treatment of her wounded soldiers. Through the press and by public speeches, Nightingale had highlighted the lack of provisioning for the wounded and advocated for much needed changes. By making nurses an integral part of the army, Canadian authorities guaranteed that their nurses would not be imitating Nightingale's example of overt criticism.

Once in England, the Canadian nurses' distinctive deep blue dress uniform and rank insignia caused quite a stir. The Canadian nurses stood out in public. They wrote of being saluted unexpectedly[13] and of being the envy of British nurses in particular for their visually distinctive uniforms. Matters did not improve when nurses of other nations learned that the Canadian nurses were also receiving officers' pay. Although not in any religious order, Canadian Great War nurses were called "nursing sisters." The veil that was an essential part of their powder blue working uniform served to accentuate the notion of separation from the men and led to them being known as "blue bells" or "ministering angels," the term preferred by the press. Their rank further separated the sisters from the wounded soldiers who were their primary patients. While nurses' rank elevated them above ordinary soldiers, all military doctors were either captains or majors and thus, just as in civil hospitals, outranked nurses and had to be obeyed. In practice, however, the nurses actually ran the wards of the hospitals in which they served. The doctors' visits could often be measured in mere minutes, but the nurses remained. The nurses' rank gave them authority over both patients and the male orderlies who worked with them and under their direct supervision on the wards.

While men usually accepted this relationship, the fact that commanding officers occasionally had to stress this reality reveals that some men did not easily accept being ordered to tasks by the nurses. The orderlies were routinely assigned to the most menial tasks, including floor sweeping, mopping, and of course, the bedpans. Later in the war, the Canadian nurses' unique status as officers was the occasion for actual friction between British and Canadian officials. In 1917, the bravery of Canadian nurses during and after the bombing of their hospitals was officially recognized with the awarding of medals. British officials refused to grant the Canadian nurses the officer level Military Cross, which was their due, and instead insisted on the Military Medal, which was awarded to non-officer ranks. Canadian officials protested but to no avail.[14]

By early 1915, it had become apparent that the initial projections of the magnitude of medical services required on the Western Front were grossly inadequate. Canada's contribution to the overall British effort that year was an increase of three general and five stationary hospitals. Originally, general hospitals were designed to house 1,000 to 1,200 patients and stationary hospitals 500 to 750 patients. As time passed, their capacities were increased, especially during the great battles. By war's end, Canada staffed and ran sixteen general hospitals scattered both in England and on the continent, and six stationary hospitals in France. The passage of time had also seen the development of four forward-area, Canadian-run casualty clearing stations (CCS) designed to provide early intervention surgical and nursing services to the wounded.[15]

Once a soldier was wounded in the forward area, whether it be in the trenches or no man's land, his unit's regimental stretcher-bearers would pick him up and move him toward treatment. Either bandaged immediately or at the advanced dressing station behind the lines, he was next moved either by hand or wheeled stretcher to a main dressing station. From the dressing station the men were transferred either by horse, motor, or tramway to the CCS, where, if required, they would receive emergency surgery. It was at the CCS that the wounded first encountered nurses. If the wounded did not require immediate surgery to save their lives, they would be placed inside a specially designed hospital train. Here again it was nurses who would care for them until their arrival many hours later at either a stationary or general hospital on the French coast. A wounded man would stay at one of these hospitals until he was stable enough to endure the transfer by ship to England and the hospital system there. A wound of sufficient severity to necessitate his transfer to England was termed a "Blighty" and was regarded as highly desirous by the men, provided the degree of severity did not mean permanent disability, such as blindness or a missing limb. If he was not injured severely enough to be sent back to England, he recovered on the French coast until he could be sent to a convalescent depot for further recuperation and strengthening before eventual return to his unit and the front. On occasion, nurses pushed back against this depersonalizing assembly line reality.[16]

This highlights one of the great disconnects of Great War medicine. Both doctors and nurses had been trained to save lives, to alleviate suffering, and to restore health, so that life, as an inherent good, could continue. At war, doctors and nurses worked to save lives so that the men could either be shipped home permanently disabled or return to the conflict to fight and to kill and to risk maiming and death again and again. Ruth Loggie's diary reveals this irony and the conflict of soul it engendered. Once patients left her care, they often wrote to her. She and the other nurses were able to follow these men's recovery and their return to their units and to danger. Sadly, later on, the diary often records their deaths. Ruth notes the news, and her repeated absence of comment speaks volumes. As nursing historian Yvonne McEwen has noted, "I have observed it is not what was said in letters, diaries, memoirs, and autobiographies; it is the unsaid that has proved to be much more interesting and worthy of further investigation."[17] Ruth's silences are indicative of an ever-evolving mixture of bewilderment, profound sadness, despair, and grief.

The war provided yet another glaring contrast to civilian nursing. At home, either in the hospitals or in private duty care, the nurses cared for patients for weeks on end, witnessing their recovery or caring for them until death. At war, there was no such continuity of care. The effective motto in the wartime hospitals of France was care until the patient could be moved, usually by ship to the hospital system in England. This was especially true just prior to and during the great battles. Orders to empty as many beds as possible, the emergency expansion of capacity, and the cancellation of staff leave, all served as undeniable harbingers of a major push at the front. During these battles, nighttime admissions followed by daytime evacuations of hundreds of patients at a time became the norm. This pattern sometimes went on for more than a week without pause, leaving the surgeons, nurses, and orderlies both mentally and physically exhausted. This was precisely Ruth's experience during the massive battles on the Somme in the summer and early autumn of 1916. The only break or relief occurred when the hospital became so full of unmoveable cases that it could receive no more wounded.

By contrast, there was also the occasional exercise of nursing discretion. Sometimes a ward came to possess a convalescing patient who required more time away from the violence and who had become very proficient as an orderly. Under these circumstances, the nurses in understaffed wards could conspire to prolong their stay.[18] These men might be hard to find when the doctors did their rounds, their recorded temperatures might run slightly higher than normal, and their recorded food intake might seem too low to merit discharge. In sum, if determined, a sympathetic nurse could conspire to keep a useful assistant in her ward for a few extra days or even weeks.

NO. 3 CANADIAN GENERAL HOSPITAL: THE MCGILL UNIT

When Ruth Loggie joined the CAMC in the spring of 1915, she signed up as part of a very specific and unique hospital unit. Ruth was one of the hand-picked nurses selected by the powers that be at McGill University medical school for service in their hospital. While difficult to grasp from our perspective, the first year of the Great War witnessed an extraordinary outpouring of both personal and institutional initiative. One striking example of this was the offer to the federal government by McGill University to establish and run a hospital as part of the CAMC. Three factors contributed to the acceptance of this offer. First, the fact that the federal government and its military officials were overwhelmed by the enormity of the task they faced in an ever expanding war effort and, as a consequence, welcomed any credible professional help that was offered. Second, due to the fame and reputation of the medical school involved, it was a very attractive offer. And third, due to the institution's extensive personal and political connections, both in Ottawa and overseas,[19] all the necessary approvals were secured very quickly. Once McGill had established the precedent, other universities soon followed suit. In just over a year, Dalhousie, Laval, Queen's, Toronto, and even St. Francis Xavier of Antigonish, Nova Scotia, an institution lacking a medical school, formed hospitals from their graduates in medicine. Eventually, the Canadian war effort would boast fully twelve hospitals that had originated as university contributions.

The initial McGill offer stipulated that the medical school would supply the doctors, nurses, and orderlies required for the hospital. Furthermore, McGill would, through private initiative, provide much of the rare, expensive, and cutting-edge technology and equipment necessary to make it a standout contribution to the Canadian war effort. This equipment included X-ray and radiation machines, supplies from the USA, and special motorized ambulance vehicles for their hospital's exclusive use. McGill insisted that it be understood and agreed upon from the outset that their hospital go as the McGill Unit and serve throughout the war as the McGill Unit, never to be broken up or to have its staff siphoned off to other hospitals.

The unique origins of No. 3 Canadian General Hospital (CGH) are amply reflected in Ruth's diary. She makes frequent references to the "unit," and her diary's pages convey her obvious pride at being a member of this select group. This context explains her regret at the transfer of original nurses, doctors, or orderlies out of the unit[20] as well as her method of chronicling the reception of nurses new to the hospital. Ruth takes pains to record whether or not the new nurses were trained at RV (Royal Victoria) or MGH (Montreal General Hospital), the two hospitals from which all the original nurses had come. Ruth also mentions the head of the medical department, Col. John McCrae, who was well regarded even before he became famous for his poem, "In Flanders Fields." (Another indication of the calibre of the staff attached to the McGill Unit is the fact that at one point it included a young Frederick Banting, who later became famous as the co-inventor of insulin.)

The McGill Unit did not just treat the wounded but strove to provide the very best treatment possible. To this end, the McGill Unit employed specially sourced imaging equipment to advance the care given. The unit's history makes frequent reference to advances made by the radiology department in providing surgeons with the exact location of bullets and shrapnel before surgery. While such aids to surgery are taken for granted in the age of computerized imaging and information sharing, a century ago this necessitated shortcuts and advances in X-ray development that were both new and cutting-edge.

No. 3 CGH arrived in Camiers, France, in July of 1915. The hospital was to be situated not in a purpose-built structure, or indeed in a building of any sort, but rather in tents on a sloping field about one mile from the ocean.[21] Here, on the windswept fields, an entire hospital complex had to be erected. As the unit history relates, "throughout July, work in preparing the hospital for patients continued, and by the 29th of the month, 55 special marquees, 19 Neilson tents, 159 bell tents, and 24 ordinary marquees had been erected."[22] Streets had to be laid out, provision made for water and sewage, housing and messes for staff, and of course wards for patients. As well, operating rooms, X-ray departments, and laboratory facilities all had to be set up in these tents. Ruth and the other nurses arrived at the site the third week of the month and commenced the work of establishing wards within the tents as well as setting up their own living quarters. The unit's first patients were received on August 7. The unit's location, so close to the sea, was ill-conceived. A great storm of wind and rain on November 13 "wrought widespread havoc,"[23] shredding canvas and flattening tents. The hospital had to be closed.

Following the storm, nurses and other staff had to be temporarily reassigned to other hospitals while an alternate site was chosen and prepared. Ruth and fifteen other nurses were transferred to the Duchess of Connaught Canadian Red Cross Hospital at Taplow in England. Thankfully, this move was temporary, for as Ruth wrote, "we seem to be rather resented and the M.D.s are none too friendly."[24] Ruth was back in France by late February, not in a field at Camiers but on the grounds of an abandoned Jesuit college in the coastal city of Boulougne. The McGill Unit's new home was a complex of old buildings and constructed huts that would eventually cover a twenty-six acre site. Ruth would remain on staff here until late August 1918. At that time she was transferred forward to No. 3 Canadian Casualty Clearing Station near Ypres, Belgium, where she would serve until late January 1919. Returning briefly to No. 3 CGH in February, Ruth was next transferred to England where she served at No. 11 Canadian General Hospital for a month before sailing home on April 4 for demobilization at Ottawa on April 13, 1919.

LIFE, LEISURE, AND RELATIONSHIPS AT NO. 3 CANADIAN GENERAL HOSPITAL

Ruth Loggie's two extant diaries record what life was like for a Canadian nurse serving in France during the Great War; however, they require both contextualization and an empathic eye. Patience and understanding are needed to see beyond the hastily written phrases, abbreviations, and cryptic references. Several overall trends can be observed. First, experiences that Ruth found initially shocking, novel, or bewildering are fully noted, but with the passage of time, she became accustomed to such experiences and they all but disappear from the diary. This was especially true of her response to the horrendous wounds inflicted on the soldiers. At first there was shock. The shock of seeing such wounds was often accompanied with a sense of amazement or pity that the soldiers were still alive.[25] With the passage of time, however, Ruth simply records the number of admissions per day with seldom a comment on their severity unless something of particular note transpired.

The diaries reflect two other general trends relative to Ruth's recording of the work she was immersed in. First is the gradual shrinkage or decline in the volume of entries made with the passage of time. For the time frame of May 6 to November 23, 1915, entries total 11,800 words; for the same time period in 1916, the total falls to just over 9,500 words.[26] Similarly, as the war drags on there is a decrease in the number and depth of "work" related entries and a corresponding increase of reporting on social or leisure activities, especially outings. This does not mean that there was less work—the exact opposite was the case. Rather it reflects the fact that her work world continued as before and required no special comment. What was recorded, however, was what she and others did in an attempt to cope with the stress and demands of that work.

As for her nursing duties, Ruth recorded what stood out to her as a professional. Arriving in France in May 1915, she was initially occupied with setting up wards in the tents at Camiers. Although not officially covered in "Instructions for CAMC Nurses,"[27] the need for nurses to create new wards became commonplace during the war. There was an ever increasing need to expand capacity to cope with the growing numbers of wounded men. Once patients arrived, Ruth comments on doing wound "dressings all day" with the result that when she wrote in her diary she was "tired and aching all over tonight."[28] Later, during a major battle, Ruth comments, "We are very busy with such enormous dressings. It is a case of eat and sleep and work these days and we are short" of staff. Again the next day, "Work still keeping ahead of us. I never get the beds made. It's dressings, dressings from morning to night."[29] At that time, Ruth's day was one of changing wound dressings on dozens of soldiers for twelve hours straight, bent over stretchers in a cramped ward with no time to even make the patients' beds. Her diary noted that the hospital received one thousand new patients that week. Ruth also mentions the practice of "specializing" several times.[30] This meant being assigned to an individual post-operative patient who was in particular danger, usually of hemorrhaging. Ruth did so for five days for a man named Freeman in October 1915. She records his hemorrhaging the first night and his delirious, disagreeable nature the next two days. She comments that while the doctor was hopeful for a recovery, the nurses were more sanguine. Sadly, Freeman hemorrhaged on the fourth day, received an intravenous drip, and then a blood transfusion direct from Captain Reford, but still died the next morning. Ruth recorded her reaction. "I feel lost and very badly in consequence but his recovery was almost too much to expect."[31]

As this incident shows, Ruth occasionally confides her mental state to her diary. In so doing, she gives us a unique glimpse into the mental health of Great War nurses immersed in a world of wounds, war, and suffering. For instance, in February 1916, just before their return to France to take up new residence at Boulogne, Ruth writes, "We feel very low in our minds about returning to France."[32] While they did not know the specifics of what their future would hold, she and her fellow nurses had already seen enough to know very well the general outlines of what lay ahead. Sure enough, on July 1, the battle of the Somme commenced and so too did the extraordinarily large trainloads of severely wounded men. By August 4, Ruth noted that the war had entered its third year, and then on August 6, "had last hours [late shift] and went to bed and wept. Such a miserable world at times."[33]

Regarding Ruth's "shifts," the daily work schedule presented another challenge with which Great War nurses had to cope. As opposed to the nurses' civilian background, in the military there was no set shift standard and very little predictability. A nurse could be moved from one ward to another from one day to the next. Ruth's diary, however, makes mention of the "night shift," which came around on a rotation and lasted for a month. On "nights," there would only be one nurse in a ward and perhaps one or two orderlies to assist her. On "days," there seems to have been at least two nurses per ward and several more orderlies. Ruth's diary further suggests that day shifts were often broken up into early and later segments with a sizeable break in the middle. The overall lack of detail has prompted nursing historian Toman "to wonder why work was the least visible aspect of their records. Perhaps they perceived it as too routine to be worth documenting or off-limits due to censorship or professional discretion."[34] Whatever the case, constantly changing shifts were yet another uncertainty with which nurses had to cope.

Ruth, typical of Great War nurses generally, coped in part by forming close bonds with her fellow nurses. Just as the correspondence of the soldiers reveals that they had close chums or mates, similar support networks and close friendships developed among nurses. This not unusually resulted in bonds that in some instances lasted a lifetime. First, there was the camaraderie of the McGill Unit itself. Ruth's sense of unit identity and of belonging was not limited to her fellow nurses, but also extended to the officers and included the doctors and fourth- and fifth-year medical students who originally served as orderlies. The diary mentions swimming excursions with fellow nurses but also attendance at sporting events, dances, costume parties, and Christmas feasts. Unlike British nurses, who were strictly forbidden from dancing, the colonial Canadians had official sanction for this physical and emotional outlet.[35] Ruth also records receiving a visit from Col. McCrae while in isolation at another hospital as she recovered from the measles.[36]

There was also the closer circle of the Montreal-trained nurses, who all shared similar backgrounds and experiences. The diary features many entries encompassing this circle of nurses. There are shopping excursions when the nurses purchased personal items or things to brighten their living quarters or items to cheer up recovering patients. These nurses could afford such things, for the Canadian Army paid them equal to men of the same rank, which "consisted of a basic $2.00 per day plus a 'messing' allowance of $1.00 per day, a field allowance while overseas of $0.60 per day, and any travel allowance due to"[37] them. This payment scheme was considerably more than they had received in civilian nursing. It allowed them, like the soldiers, to assign a portion of their pay to be sent home to family in Canada.[38]

Indeed the prominence given to outings to the countryside and quick trips whenever possible could give a casual reader the mistaken impression that the nurses devoted a disproportionate amount of time to such activities. Instead, their prominence is indicative of the nurses availing themselves of one of the few distractions and coping mechanisms available. The nurses needed a break, an escape from wounds and suffering, and these outings, whether short walks, bicycle trips, or bus rides, served the need. The usual companions on such outings were the nurses who dwelt in the same hut (they were housed in pairs) and those who were off-duty at the time.

Under the stress of war, all was not continually harmonious within the nurses' world. Ruth is not hesitant to confide to her diary her frustration, impatience, and even anger. Soon after their initial arrival in France and while temporarily posted to No.1 Canadian General Hospital, Ruth records spending a day sewing burlap onto the floor of a service tent—"a thankless job." Tellingly, the officer commanding (O.C.) characterized the effort as "a useless waste of time and material." Overhearing the comment, the unit's matron commented to Ruth that "one gets used to such appreciation in army life."[39] The matron at No. 1 Canadian General Hospital, although for the moment Ruth's immediate superior, did not escape Ruth's ire. Ruth had harsh words for her during the early days in France. Regarding the reception of patients in early June, Ruth commented, "Such poor management. One couldn't fancy anything worse than the management staff here in every way. A disgrace to Canada. The Matron absolutely useless and not even ladylike, the doctors are such a poor class of men."[40] The next day Ruth again confides to her diary, "If Canadians knew the manner of the in-charge people they are paying here, they would never stand for it. Col McLancer, the O. C. from St. John, is like a man in his dotage and Matron Nesbit is surely quite a bit 'off.' It's a joke till patients are involved."[41] Again a few days later, Ruth, not being alone in her anger and frustration, noted, "We really think a protest or report should be made in some quarters. She is surely batty."[42] Apparently the matron was the topic of conversation among the nurses, and disparaging comments were not uncommon.[43] It is at this point in her diary that Ruth records various daily postings by Matron Nesbit, the purpose being to demonstrate her unprofessionalism and incompetence.

As Ruth's comments illustrate, it was not just the matron but also the O.C. who came in for particular criticism. It appears that Ruth's sentiments were not entirely hidden, for on July 20 she records, "Got a 'call down' from the O.C. for spoiling the patients and for talking back. He certainly is a disgrace to Canada and to Saint John particularly." Tensions continued the next month when the nurses had been promised use of the car for an excursion only to learn that "the O.C. had taken it so our trip was off. We went to bed <u>mad</u> and spent a miserable sleepless day."[44] It must be noted that Ruth's severe criticism of Matron Nesbit coincided with the McGill nurses' first exposure to large influxes of severely wounded soldiers to a hospital in France.

It is also true that the McGill nurses were outside of their unit and under the command of others. How much this influenced their willingness to criticize is difficult to determine, but there are no such overt criticisms of the administration of the McGill Unit's matron or O.C.

Given the circumstances, tensions unsurprisingly were not limited to conflicts with those in authority. Sometimes even fellow nurses were the cause of anger. When it was time to move from No. 1 Canadian General Hospital to their own unit, Ruth relates that she returned to her room from duty only to find "my trunk packed by Buchanan," who appears to have been all too ready to see Ruth go. Not surprisingly, Ruth noted that this "made me furious."[45] Ruth also recorded the generally cool reception that the McGill nurses received from their fellow Canadians during their brief stay at Taplow in December 1915: "we seem to be resented."[46]Again at Taplow, in early January 1916, "The OC and Matron visited our Ward this morning and the OC said that the beds looked as though the wrath of God had struck them."[47] Their return to France the next month, although tinged with trepidation, was at least a release from the atmosphere of Taplow.

CLARE GASS: A CLOSE FRIEND AND CONFIDANTE

Ruth Loggie's closest friend by far was fellow Maritimer, nurse, and McGill graduate, Clare Gass. A native of Shubenacadie, Nova Scotia, Clare's father owned a general store and had interests in the lumber business. This resourcefulness permitted the family's oldest child and only daughter to attend boarding school at Edgehill in Windsor, Nova Scotia. After Edgehill,

Clare entered the nursing program at Montreal General Hospital, graduating two years after Ruth, in 1912. While Ruth's close circle of nurse friends included fellow New Brunswickers Christina Watling of Chatham and Elizabeth Lillian Dickie of River Charlo, the diary makes clear that Clare Gass was her closest friend.

Fortunately, their friendship is evidenced not only in Ruth's surviving diary, but also in Clare's diary. Clare Gass's diary commences March 4, 1915, and extends all the way to December 1918. It starts with an entry concerning the imminent departure of the McGill Unit from Quebec and concludes with Clare's return to Halifax. It is thus explicitly a war diary. Ruth's diary starts when the McGill Unit boards ship in Quebec City and ends abruptly on November 23, 1916. Thus Ruth's diary is also a record of her war experience but one that ends abruptly for reasons discussed below.

Ruth's diary records that she, Clare, Lill (Dickie), and Watling were cabin mates on the journey overseas. During the month of June, Ruth mentions Clare fifteen times in her diary, and Clare reciprocates fifteen times in her own. Indeed, a synoptic examination of the two diaries for the entire period of overlap reveals a similar pattern. The two nurse friends mention one another in their respective diaries over 150 times each. This dual coverage of the same events can be most informative and revealing. To cite only one instance, Clare reveals that the names Sunderland and Clark that appear in Ruth's diary in the autumn of 1916 are two ex-patient admirers of Ruth and that Sunderland is an Australian and Clark is an Englishman. Clare finds the two men "very interesting from a physiological point of view."[48]

Initially, at Étaples, Ruth and Clare roomed together in a tent; later, at Camiers, Ruth and Dickie were roommates in a prefabricated "Nissen" hut. Although Ruth and Clare never went on leave at the same time, their friendship is clearly evidenced by the fact that Ruth wrote Clare three times while away on a fourteen-day leave with Dickie and Watling in 1916.[49] They were close friends, pals, and confidantes. They shared similar family backgrounds, were both graduates of Montreal General Hospital, and were members of the McGill Unit. They also had male family members serving in the Canadian Expeditionary Force. Both diaries are filled with references to their serving family members' whereabouts, their visits, and their well-being.[50] For instance, Clare's brother Cyril visited while on leave in April 1916. He had a friend with him whom Ruth "took with me so Clare could have Cyril to herself." Later, Cyril sustained a foot wound and subsequently lost a portion of his lower leg to amputation. Clare's much younger brother, Blanchard, also visited several times but was killed at Vimy Ridge in April 1917. Ruth's brother Leonard served with the 26th Battalion and survived the war. Ruth's cousin Murray Anderson suffered a serious shrapnel wound to the chest serving with the 6 CMR at the Battle of Mount Sorrel in June 1916. He too survived to return to Canada.

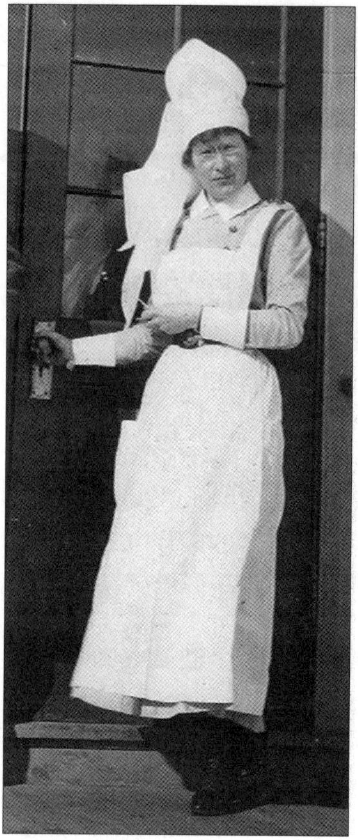

Ruth's best friend, Clare Gass, in working uniform, France, circa 1916.

Ruth and Clare seldom worked together, but they took every opportunity to spend their leisure hours together. Mostly they went on excursions, which often involved the use of bicycles they bought in France. It is here that we encounter one of the most strikingly novel aspects of Ruth's diary—her amazingly diverse and extensive vocabulary of travelling verbs! In Ruth's telling, she and Clare walked, biked, explored, strolled, tramped, bused, taxied, motored, were detailed, rode, wheeled, and toured. At one point she even appears to have attempted to say "Forded" when they had an opportunity to travel in a Ford automobile! The most interesting term is "tramping," which appears to be a New Brunswick idiom.[51] Clare Gass, a Nova Scotian, never uses the term. The verb is employed when the excursion described is of a particularly rambling, exploratory nature, as in seeking out edible mushrooms[52] or when exploring previously unseen countryside.[53]

Ruth's diary ends abruptly after the entry for November 23, 1916. Clare's diary continues until her return to Canada months after the Armistice. Given the extraordinary extent of parallel entries concerning each other, one would think that Clare's diary would contain an explanation as to why Ruth's diary ends as it does. Sadly, this is not the case. While Clare records Ruth's admirers, illnesses, and even headaches, her diary also falls silent on November 23 and does not contain a single entry until December 16, a full three-week silence. When Clare does recommence writing, all she talks about are Christmas preparations. She states that she and Ruth are both busy getting parcels ready for men at the front and preparing for the observance of Christmas on their respective wards. The absence of entries in Clare's diary as well as Ruth's suggests that the cause was something that affected both Clare and Ruth equally. The unit war diary reveals a large number of admissions and evacuations during this period, combined with a high degree of illness among the hospital's staff. In the period of Clare's silence following the ending of Ruth's diary, six staff nurses were admitted to No. 14 General Hospital with illnesses. Added to this is the unit diary's notation that fully twenty-three NCOs and orderlies were admitted to hospital in the month of November. On top of all this, one doctor resigned in order to return to Canada, and Col. McCrae was granted three weeks' sick leave. It appears the most likely explanation of Ruth's diary containing no more entries for 1916 is that she was simply too busy and too tired to make them. Clare's three-week silence confirms the generalized nature of this as the most plausible cause. While Clare did eventually finish out the year with a few brief entries, Ruth ceased to make any further diary entries in 1916.

If Ruth did have a diary for 1917 or 1918, it has not come down to us. Even if such documents ever existed, they would be like those of her friend Clare: small, scant, and brief. Clare's extant diary for 1917 is a small pocket notebook with less than half the words of 1916. Entries are fewer and briefer. The days and periods lacking any diary entries increase noticeably. Clare's 1917 was a year filled with grief, as she lost both a brother and her cousin. One index as to how much things have changed is that until her transfer forward in November to a CCS, Ruth Loggie is mentioned a total of only nine times. As for Clare's 1918 diary, it is only one-third the size of that for 1917. The desire for keeping a diary is gone. It is as if words can no longer contain or convey what lived experience has become. For her part, Ruth's file reveals that she went on leave twice in 1917 and once in 1918 before she too was sent forward to a CCS in August of 1918. She continued at the CCS until January 1919, at which time she returned briefly to No. 3 CGH, took a two-week leave, and then began her journey back to Canada. Ruth Loggie was demobilized at Ottawa on April 13, 1919. Her war had come to an end.

A NOTE ON THE TEXT OF RUTH LOGGIE'S DIARY

I would like to thank Barbara Wilson for permission to use her typewritten transcript of both of Ruth Loggie's extant diaries. In the autumn of 2017, Barbara gave Ruth's original 1915 diary to the Provincial Archives of New Brunswick for safekeeping.[54] Ruth's original 1916 diary is in the care of the Historical Committee of the Burnt Church and New Jersey Senior Citizens Group Inc. Both volumes were commercially purchased diaries complete with days and dates printed on the pages. They were hardcover volumes roughly the size of the book you are presently handling. Physically, the two diaries are in quite different condition. The 1915 volume has come apart and exists as single-page sheets within the hardcovers of the original book. There are several pressed tree leaves and one dried flower between the unused initial pages of the diary. The 1916 volume is still intact as a book without loose pages. This volume, when opened, displays a week's worth of entries at a glance. I have consulted the originals of both volumes in the preparation of the following text. While my goal has been to replicate the original as faithfully as possible, certain concessions have had to be made to promote readability and comprehension. This has meant the spelling out of words and the occasional expansion of clipped entries into comprehensible phrases. When an individual initially appears in the diary, either by first name or nickname, I identify them fully in an endnote. I abstain from repeating this information in further entries. An introductory list of the people mentioned most often (the Cast of Characters, page 31) seeks to aid the reader in their identification. Given the host of persons mentioned, almost always by first name only, it has proven impossible to identify them all. Even if it were possible, the sheer volume of notations would become a distraction from the actual text. I trust I have sufficiently identified the main characters. I have not changed American, British, or Canadian spelling of words so as not to alter the flavour of Ruth's text. I have, however, adjusted punctuation and abbreviations if deemed necessary for purposes of clarity. I have also standardized Ruth's frequent misspelling and various spellings of local place names. As Ruth neither spoke nor wrote French, her diary often includes her guesswork as to the proper French spelling of place names other terms. The goal has been to employ present-day usage so that the reader can follow her travels on a good map or, even better, on Google Maps.

Throughout, I have consulted Susan Mann's scholarly text of Clare Gass's war diary for the wonderful opportunity of further contextualization that it provides. All references to Clare's diary are from Mann's work, but for consistency between texts, I have chosen to cite passages primarily by date rather than by page number. I would also direct readers to Cynthia Toman's excellent *Sister Soldiers of the Great War: The Nurses of the Canadian Army Medical Corps*. Beyond these excellent scholarly aids, what I hope this work communicates is the Great War experience of a remarkable Canadian: Nursing Sister Ruth Loggie, of Burnt Church, New Brunswick.

NOTES

1 Available online at Library and Archives Canada (LAC) are six nurses' accounts of their Great War experiences. One is an account written after the events, two are sets of letters, and three are diaries. Andrea McKenzie describes all of these, save the Alice Isaacson diary, as "scanty and fragmentary" (McKenzie, War-Torn Exchanges, 220n10). Cynthia Toman lists many more nurses' records in her work, but sadly the majority of them can be given the same characterization. Still, Toman's work is laudable for she has revealed the potential inherent in the unearthing of family records even if many remain, for the time being, privately held and/or unpublished.

2 An indeterminate number of Canadian women also served overseas as nurses with other nations and organizations. Additionally, approximately five hundred Canadian women served overseas as Volunteer Aid Detachment (VAD) workers in British institutions. See Quiney, This Small Army of Women.

3 Only four Canadian nurses published written accounts of their wartime experiences. They wrote at different times, independent of each other, and unaware that any other nurse had committed her experiences to writing. Constance Bruce published Humour in Tragedy in 1918. Mabel Clint published Our Bit in 1934, just five years before her death. Much later, in 1977, Maude Wilkinson's account appeared in Canadian Nurse and was later published as Four Score and Ten. Finally, in 1981, Katherine Wilson-Simmie's Lights Out was published. She was ninety-four at the time.

4 See Macphail, Official History of the Canadian Forces in the Great War. See also Toman, Sister Soldiers of the Great War, 6.

5 See McEwen, In The Company of Nurses, 182.

6 Ruth Loggie diary (RLD), June 5, 1915. As Yvonne McEwen observed "the nurses on the Western Front…very quickly came to realize there was no equivalent in civilian nursing that could have prepared them for the traumas of military engagements" (McEwen, 94).

7 Toman, Sister Soldiers, 28.

8 The frequency of reference in the text to nurses with the prefix "Mrs." can be attributed to the fact that some women did not reveal their marital status at enlistment while others married secretly after signing up. See Toman, 50.

9 Toman, 39.

10 Joined by a River, 82.

11 Heritage Canadiana, Military HQ Rank and Pay, file T-17636, image 173. Available at canada.ca/en/services/defence/caf/militaryhistory.

12 Toman, Sister Soldiers, 15.

13 Hebb, In Their Own Words, 110. Also Mann, War Diary of Clare Gass, 59.

14 Toman, Sister Soldiers, 214.

15 Toman, Appendix B.

16 Moved by a soldier's patient suffering, in her entry for July 6, 1915, Clare Gass mentions securing a patient's transfer back to England so as to see his family, even though his wound was slight (Mann, War Diary of Clare Gass, 39).

17 McEwen, In the Company of Nurses, 4.

18 Clint, Our Bit: Memories of War Service, 75.

19 H. S. Birkett, McGill's dean of medicine, had ties to federal militia minister Sir Sam Hughes, and in England, Sir William Osler of Oxford University, formerly of McGill, had access to key figures at the War Office in London,

including Sir Alfred Keogh, the Director General of British Army Medical Services (Fetherstonhaugh, No. 3 Canadian General Hospital, 4–7).

20 RLD, Nov. 12, 1915.

21 Sanitary Department Report, November 1915, No. 3 CGH Unit Diary, LAC, MIKAN 2005099, Item 41.

22 Fetherstonhaugh, No. 3 CGH, 20.

23 Fetherstonhaugh, 35.

24 RLD, Dec. 11, 1915.

25 Early on, Ruth notes, "Kerr, a Highland lad, has practically his face blown away and his body is untouched. It is too cruel" (RLD, June 19, 1915).

26 A similar pattern can be observed in Clare Gass's published diary, wherein the number and volume of entries declines with each year. There are eighty-six pages of text in 1915, sixty-four in 1916, thirty in 1917, and a mere thirteen for all of 1918.

27 Reproduced in Mann, War Diary of Clare Gass, 215–24.

28 RLD, July 2, 1915.

29 RLD, Sept. 30, 1915.

30 RLD, Oct. 31, 1915; May 8, 1916.

31 RLD, Nov. 5, 1915.

32 RLD, Feb. 4, 1915.

33 RLD, Aug. 6, 1916.

34 Toman, Sister Soldiers, 74.

35 Toman, 163–4.

36 RLD, May 6, 1916.

37 Toman, Sister Soldiers, 17.

38 Records reveal that Ruth assigned $40.00 per month to her sister Rachael back in Burnt Church, NB.

39 RLD May 29, 1915.

40 RLD June 4, 1915.

41 RLD June 5, 1915.

42 RLD June 9, 1915.

43 Ruth's friend Clare Gass expressed similar frustrations and criticism. See Mann, War Diary of Clare Gass, 27.

44 RLD Aug. 20, 1915.

45 RLD July 23, 1915.

46 RLD Dec. 11, 1915.

47 RLD Jan. 3, 1916.

48 Mann, War Diary of Clare Gass, 146.

49 Mann, 123–4.

50 Clare had four brothers who served: Cyril, Gerald, Athelstan, and Blanchard. Tragically, Clare lost both her younger brother Blanchard and a cousin, Laurence Gass, in the Battle of Vimy Ridge in April of 1917 (Mann, War Diary of Clare Gass, 287 n12).

51 See fellow New Brunswicker Pauline Ballock's usage in Hebb, In Their Own Words, Sept. 3, 8, and 9, 1917.

52 RLD Sept. 28, 1916.

53 RLD June 13 and Nov. 2, 1915.

54 Reference number is PANB MC 4183, MS1 "Ruth Loggie Diary."

Ruth Loggie's CAMC Timeline

APRIL 22, 1915:	Joins CAMC in Montreal
MAY 6, 1915:	Sails from Montreal onboard RMS *Metagama*
MAY 28, 1915:	No. 1 Canadian General Hospital (Étaples, France)
JULY 23, 1915:	No. 3 CGH (Camiers, France)
DECEMBER 8, 1915:	Duchess of Connaught Canadian Red Cross Hospital (Taplow, England)
FEBRUARY 19, 1916:	No. 3 CGH (Boulogne, France)
APRIL 24–MAY 6, 1916:	No. 14 General Hospital (Wimereux, France); sick with measles
MAY 30–JUNE 12, 1916:	On leave from No. 3 CGH

MARCH 13–27, 1917:	On leave from No. 3 CGH
AUGUST 31–SEPT. 13, 1917:	On leave from No. 3 CGH
JUNE 24–JULY 6, 1918:	On leave from No. 3 CGH
AUGUST 26, 1918:	No. 3 Canadian Casualty Clearing Station
JANUARY 19, 1919:	No. 3 CGH
FEB. 17–MARCH 3, 1919:	On leave from No. 3 CGH
MARCH 8, 1919:	CAMC Casualty Company (Shorncliffe, England)
MARCH 10, 1919:	Returning Draft Transport Depot
MARCH 10–APRIL 3, 1919:	No. 11 CGH (Shorncliffe)
APRIL 3, 1919:	Sails to Canada on SS *Lapland*
APRIL 13, 1919:	Discharged at M.O. District Depot No. 4 (Ottawa)

Cast of Characters

(INDIVIDUALS FREQUENTLY MENTIONED IN RUTH'S DIARY)

MISS BRAND OR BRANDIE: Louise J. Brand, a Nova Scotia–born McGill nurse

CLARE: Clare Gass, Ruth's closest nurse friend

GILLIS OR LOU: Louella Louise Gillis, a New Brunswick–born McGill nurse

GRAY: Lilly Naomi Gray, a Montreal-born McGill nurse

HELEN: Helen (Loggie) Donald, Ruth's cousin and friend who wrote her often

KERR: Kerr Loggie, a soldier from Chatham, NB, a distant cousin to Ruth

LAPP: Victor Lapp, a former McGill student and orderly

LAURA: Laura M. Anderson, Ruth's cousin and friend living in Burnt Church, NB

LILL OR DICKIE: E. Lillian Dickie, a close nurse friend from River Charlo, NB

LEN: Leonard Loggie, Ruth's soldier brother

MCCONNELL: Rachael McConnell, an Irish-born McGill nurse

MCGREER: Louise McGreer, a Montreal-born McGill nurse

MURRAY: Murray Anderson, Ruth's cousin

MISS NICHOLS: Florence Nichols, an Ontario-born nurse

RAY OR RAE: Rachael Loggie, Ruth's close sister and confidante

STEEL(E): Mary F. Steele, a McGill graduate nurse

STEVIE: Louise Myrtle Stevens, a Nova Scotia–born nurse

SUNDERLAND: Edward H. Sunderland (AEF), Ruth's Australian soldier admirer

TATE: Annette Tate, a Jamaica-born nurse

TINI OR WATLING: Christina Mary Watling, a close nurse friend from Chatham, NB

WARRIE: Warren P. Loggie, a soldier brother to Kerr and a distant cousin to Ruth

The War Diary of Ruth Loggie

1915

Ruth sails for England with the rest of No. 3 Canadian General Hospital, the McGill Unit, in early May 1915. The crossing exposes Ruth to the realities of military life. "Mufti" or civilian dress soon becomes entirely forbidden and uniforms the order of the day. As for orders, they become commonplace, direct, and serious. When an officer from another unit "pretends" to drill the nurses, they are informed in no uncertain terms that only their McGill officers are entitled to direct drill. Both ship-wide blackouts and lifebelts (lifejackets) become obligatory. Once they reach English waters, the Royal Navy escorts make Ruth feel very secure; however, upon landing and learning of the Lusitania's *sinking, the need for the precautions becomes obvious. Having been on the water at the same time as twelve hundred people died casts a pall of reality over the excitement of the voyage overseas. The war is very real.*

Even in London, with all the sights and sounds to take in, the fact that they are in the army is brought home. Although these women are graduate nurses and many, like Ruth, have been employed for years in private duty or in hospitals in large cities, they now have to be "looked after" while in London by a male escort of three officers. Despite this period paternalism, Ruth and her friends do not let their mandated chaperones dampen their enjoyment of the great city.

THURSDAY, MAY 6

Came on board at 7:30 a.m. *Metagama* and sailed at 11 a.m. Were given a wonderful send off and the day was perfect. Passed Quebec this evening. It looked splendid and familiar. Watling, Lill, Clare[1] and I have a cabin together. Keeping our trunks in our room.

FRIDAY, MAY 7

Another bright day and we are so comfortable in mufti.[2] Breakfast and lunch are informal but we dress for dinner and go down in order. Getting colder as we get into the Gulf. Are all delighted Miss Duncan[3] is to be our Matron's assistant—a wise appointment. Miss Davies[4] is in charge of the operating room. Lots of music on board, brass band and bagpipes belonging to the 21st[5]—usual ship's orchestra. Very cold. Usual inspection in a.m. & drill at 11 a.m.

SATURDAY, MAY 8

Tug of war between nursing sisters; Vics and Generals.[6] Generals win. Passed Cape Race this a.m. so this is our last sight of land. Lively time on the deck this evening, marching behind the bagpipes. Promptly stopped by our Col. Also "Thou shalt not wear mufti" posted, so good bye comfort. Also none but our own officers are allowed to drill us. Hard times.

SUNDAY, MAY 9

Very cold. Number of icebergs, as many as six at a time. Two about a mile away. Men say one 250 ft above the water, top covered by cloud. Communion early this a.m. and service on deck at 10:30. Nearly froze to death. Dickie[7] detailed for 6 hr. duty to appendix case operated on yesterday by Col. Elder. Clare's swallow returning today. Armitage very ill and Handcock[8] miserable. I am fine and dandy. No drills or inspection today.

MONDAY, MAY 10

Not so cold. Inspection as usual at 9:30 and Drill later on. Lots of seasickness. Sports on lower deck in afternoon, pillow fights, potato races, etc. Winners to race tomorrow. Looking very stormy and beginning to rain. McGill officers had party among themselves. Col. Yates birthday. Steamer sighted flying French flag. Messages received but no answer given by our Capt. He then changed course for a time.

TUESDAY, MAY 11

A rainy day and quite a wind but the boat is steady and most of the sick are feeling better and are on deck. I was orderly nurse for the day, Dickie on duty as usual 6–12 p.m. Patient is fine but so tired of the motion. Inspection and drill as usual. Caps allowed during drill. Pillow fight by the 21st Battalion. Sports among the officers. Our men are too much afraid of their dignity to join.

WEDNESDAY, MAY 12

Life boat drill at 10:30. Told each to keep our own belt in future. Very rough today and vacancies at table numerous. Armitage and Handcock very ill yet. Matron MacLatchy[9] ill all the way.

Raining most of the day. No band out in the evening and few people out on deck. Concert posted, but postponed on account of the weather.

THURSDAY, MAY 13

No inspection or drill, lots of miserable people yet. Sea not so rough and a bright clear day. Land not sighted yet. The concert came off this evening, a great success (20£ made). No lights on deck tonight, port holes darkened with paper and we sleep in underwear with great coats, life belts, and caps ready. Twelve life boats are hung ready and ladders in coils at proper places.

FRIDAY, MAY 14

The sea very much populated. Wrote seven letters in between running to look at vessels. At nightfall, five torpedo boat destroyers quietly appeared from nowhere. Great excitement on our ship. We watched the signaling from our decks and went to bed feeling very safe. Not much sleep though as the girls were very noisy.

SATURDAY, MAY 15

Docked at Plymouth at 4:30 a.m. A glorious morning but turned out rainy later on. Had lunch on board and then took the train to London. Col. Elder, Major Howard, and Capt. Hutchison looking after us. The remainder of our unit and the 21st go to Shorncliffe. At 7 p.m. we put up at Premier Hotel, Southhampton Row. Sent a cable. Hope they get it before Sunday. Terrible news of the *Lusitania* and we heard report that a report had reached here that we were torpedoed. Col. Birkett called Principal Peterson of our arrival (for publication).

SUNDAY, MAY 16

Watling, Dickie, and I went to Regent Sq. Presbyterian Church in a.m. Dickie not feeling well and stayed in after lunch. Watling and I went to Intercession Service in the Abbey. After dinner a number of us started out, and Clare and I got separated and took two long bus rides home. Saw the search lights at work. Home at 11 p.m. Dickie thought we were lost. Hotel fare not up to much here.

MONDAY, MAY 17

Watling, Dickie, and I went to Canadian Red Cross to inquire for Alex.[10] He is in hospital near Torquay. Went to Westminster Abbey and took lunch in Charing Cross and went by bus to Tower of London. Coming home we got lost, but got in for dinner. At 7:45 p.m. got word to go to France tomorrow at 7:15 a.m. Dickie goes to Clivedon, England, and Watling stops here. My luggage has just gone. Thirty-five of us go to France to 1st Canadian Hospital.

After only a few days in London, the Canadian nurses are dispatched to various hospitals. Ruth is among a group sent to France immediately. This quick dispersal of the recently arrived Canadian nursing resource indicates just how great the British need for nurses is on the Western Front.[11] They arrive at the coastal French city of Boulogne, a place which is to figure prominently in the McGill Unit's future. Ruth's initial impressions must always be kept in mind; she finds the city dirty, busy, and noisy. The port city of Boulogne is the major entry and exit point for the British Empire's war effort on the Western Front. There, activity never ceases. Hundreds of thousands of troops arrive through this port, and over the course of the war, hundreds of thousands of wounded men will depart. This windswept, sand-duned section of the French coast surrounding Boulogne will become home to many wartime hospitals over the next three years. Ruth will walk, tour, bike, and tramp the surrounding countryside seeking new vistas but also solace and escape from the agonies and toils of war. In her diary, Clare tells us Ruth actually fears getting lost among the rolling, repetitive dunes,[12] but the countryside itself brings Ruth solace. The other thing that gives her a break and brings her relief are letters from home. Ruth receives her first such letter while in France on May 29. The first wounded arrive in her ward on May 31. Ruth's war "somewhere in France" has begun.

TUESDAY, MAY 18

Left London in the rain, a miserable cold storm. Crossed from Folkstone to Boulogne—a cold trip. Are put up at the Grand Hotel de Louvre in a dirty, dusty room. Clare, Watters,[13] McGreer,[14] and me. A quartette of miserable women. This town is taken over by the British, and nearly every vehicle has a red cross on it. Thousands of troops pass through here every night on way to the front. Saw Upton[15] today. She is at No. 1 Stationary Hospital three miles away. We are thirty-five miles from the front line here.

WEDNESDAY, MAY 19

Went out to take tea with Col. McKee at No. 1 Stationary. The hospital is lovely, all tents pitched among the daisies and buttercups. Upton, Galt,[16] & Pelletier[17] fine and fat and happy. We walked home in time for dinner. This is the noisiest place I ever struck, trains and ambulances just below our window, and the train whistles are screams. The weather is spring, not much earlier than ours. We hope to get settled by the end of the week.

Clare and Ruth on an excursion in France.

THURSDAY, MAY 20

Beautiful warm day. Clare and I discovered a cathedral and had a lovely walk on the ramparts before lunch. Watling and companions arrived on their way to Rouen. They leave tomorrow at noon. Miss Archibald and Mrs. Austin went to Rouen today.[18] The stream of wounded is steady from the ambulances to the hospital ships. Took tea at No. 1 Stationary with matron. Col. Finley & Capt. Shanks there to meet us, both fine and so talkative. Alex Watling doing well and will soon return to the trenches.

FRIDAY, MAY 21

Morning orders. No sister to leave hotel. Breakfast in bed and watch the transfer of wounded to hospital ship, which lies just by our window. Kept in all afternoon till late waiting for a telegram from OC giving our matron permission to loan us to the Imperial hospital for the day. Clare and I shopped, bought creton, cups and saucers, and hooks. Had a jolly time. Watling and her bunch left for Rouen.

SATURDAY, MAY 22

Left Boulogne for Étaples at 11 a.m. Beautiful day and a perfect ride through the country. No. 1 Stationary Hospital just being formed, three others nearby. Mr. Archibald here. Had the surprise of my life when he said "Hello, Sister Loggie." So glad to see him.[19] Dr. Kenneth Cameron and McKenzie Forbes here, busy putting up tents. Letter from Dickie today. Having a fine time in England. It is perfect here. We are in huts and Clare and I have ours cozy already, and we are all as happy as larks.

SUNDAY, MAY 23

A perfectly beautiful day. Army service at 10:30. McGreer and Woods[20] on duty in operating room unpacking things. Work of putting up tents continues today. Had a nice nap after dinner, tea at 4 p.m., and a number of officers in courtesy calls. We went touring after supper up over the sand dunes. Rather a pretty view from the tops, but this part is not pretty. The cultivated spots being used for building sites. The stretch of water to the front of us just an overflow from the sea.

MONDAY, MAY 24

A hot day. We walked to Paris Plage four miles away. Most of the shops closed so shopping was a failure. Saw Dr. Johnston on our way. Paris Plage is a fashionable watering place and has a good beach. Seven of us hired a motor to bring us home, but we were set out on a road quite half a mile from here and it was a swift work getting home for prompt dinner. Went for a lovely walk in the evening and discovered a lovely brook and heard some rare bird singing, including a cuckoo. Saw an airship flying toward the north.

TUESDAY, MAY 25

Another hot day. July weather at home and we are not very suitably clothed. Clare and I walked into Étaples and shopped. We carried home two books, two straw mats, a lantern, a glass vase. Also went to see an old church built by the English in 1004, now a R.C. church. Quite worth another visit. The Matron and Sister Eastwood[21] gone to Boulogne to meet the other sisters. Sewed tapes and tent ropes. A dusty bunch of girls arrived in p.m. Made beds after supper.

WEDNESDAY, MAY 26

Sewed tapes and made dressings and supplies. Saw Mr. Archibald at a distance and Dr. Losier for a minute. Clare and I detailed to get tea—some work. Made jam sandwiches and thin b. and b. and endless cups of tea. Several officers in. After supper, Tate[22] and Shephard and I went to the brook. Tate and I waded and washed our feet. Got some mint and mignonettes.

THURSDAY, MAY 27

Posted for ward "C" with Miss McIntosh.[23] Tate also. Hut ward with accommodations for twenty patients—all stretcher cases. Will be glad to get to work. Fitting up the ward goes on slowly. Hard to get requisitions filled. After supper, Clare and I went walking, discovered a large residence. A Castle we call it, tucked away behind the dunes. Came home through them and saw millions of rabbits. The first living things I have seen.

FRIDAY, MAY 28

Cold day. I scrubbed tables etc. and washed dishes, hemmed towels most of the day. Army life is queer. Major Le Bel our O.C. ward; Capt. Hunt and Capt. Ramsay his assistants.

The Major is French and fat but means work and has had experience in the Imperial Service. After dinner we went through a Red Cross train lying on the track. Very nice and airy and clean. Went for a walk along the track and came home by No. 18 Hospital. They are receiving there. Train load just arrived. Letters from Laura[24] and Frances H.

SATURDAY, MAY 29

Cold day. Sewed burlap to floor service tent. A thankless job. O.C. said useless waste of material and time. The Matron says one gets used to such appreciation in army life. Service tent moved second time by O.C.'s order. Dinner late, matron unpunctual & kept us in Ante Tent after which made our walk late. Went back along the Boulogne road. So pretty there. The hawthorn hedges still in bloom. Passed the "castle" again. Came home by No. 18 Hospital and got to bed at once. Cold night.

SUNDAY, MAY 30

On duty. Service by Presbyterian minister at 10 a.m. Had sham receiving of patients. To drill the orderlies and nurses. Received three orderlies carried in for the purpose. Off duty at 1:30.

MONDAY, MAY 31

Walked to Paris Plage after duty. Had supper at La Chat Blue. Walked home and went on duty to receive our first patients. About fifty were admitted. "C" ward getting five, no serious wounds. Just two or three Canadians in the lot.

As mentioned in the introduction, Ruth's diary replicates examples of what she and the other nurses found to be petty or officious pronouncements by No. 1 CGH's matron, Violet Claire Nesbitt. The examples below all appear in Ruth's diary at the end of May and early June 1915. The underlined insistence on punctuality and the threat to give away a portion of a nurse's wardrobe strike Ruth as entirely overdone. They are no longer trainees in a Canadian hospital but professional nurses at war. As for the insistence on cape flaps and not using chin straps, the matron is undoubtedly correct. All CAMC nurses would have received prior instruction on such matters. Ruth's disapproval is no doubt connected to the threat of future consequences should such infringements persist. Ruth saw the matron's reaction as wholly disproportionate to the matter at issue. Particular touches to uniforms do not affect the performance, efficiency, and professionalism of the care the individual nurse provided. It is, however, true that in addition to the usual personnel files, unit matrons are also tasked with keeping highly confidential files on each nurse. These files are to include evaluations of attitude, compliance, demeanour, and dependability as well as nursing ability and professionalism. Unfortunately for the historian, theses files have not survived. The last two entries indicate that the matron is aware that her nurses are not willing to accept her postings without comment. Indeed, they indicate both a degree of pushback as well as the frustration of a matron struggling to manage those under her charge.

NOTICE:
The charge nurses will please assemble in the Matron's office administration building at 8:15 sharp.

If these garments are not claimed this evening they will be sold for the Red Cross fund.

(Said garments were two shirts and a handkerchief owned by one of the Nursing Sisters.)

Irregularities in uniforms are still consistently being carried out by the sisters of No. 1 Canadian General Hospital such as capes being worn with flaps inside. What has been allowed by other hospitals will not be allowed in No. 1. There ought to be no confusion as it is to be supposed that all C.A.M.C. Sisters were properly instructed regarding these matters sometime or other.

Straps under the chin are forbidden by the Matron in chief and have no authorized precedent.

Sisters are warned that the constant infringement of these rules will mitigate greatly against them in the course of time.

POSTED:
Sister Bell will report for duty in the supply room and remain on duty till notified to do otherwise. (Poor Bell)

NOTICE:
Nursing Sisters are to read notices intelligently and not ask useless questions which seem dear to their hearts. Signed: Matron

Would the Sisters please understand that all letters are to be left open. The censor told me this afternoon that sisters Gilles & Chisholm's[25] letters were sealed. I suggest a trefine[26] applied to your skull. Signed: Matron

Early June exposes Ruth and the other nurses of the McGill Unit who are temporarily stationed at No. 1 CGH to the terrible wounds inflicted in the battles of the Great War. On June 5 she notes that the men are "so badly cut up"; two days later she mentions "terrible wounds," and on June 19 comments on "a Highland lad [who] has practically his face blown away and his body untouched." Alongside her initial exposure to such horrendous wounds, and no doubt in part a response to them, is her disgust and overt criticism of those in charge at No. 1 CGH. While it is indeed rare to encounter such pointed criticism in the written record, Ruth is not alone in her views. Her friend Clare Gass also describes the hospital management as "an abomination" and characterizes the OC as "a doting old idiot" and the Matron as "surely mentally unbalanced."[27] *Living under such circumstances explains their frequent excursions to Étaples and their long walks, for only then is there "a rest from this atmosphere." On the lighter side, Ruth also experiences a "small world" moment when one of the patients turns out to be a clerk from Goodwin's, a Montreal department store where she used to shop.*

TUESDAY, JUNE 1

Such a funny day. So much hurry and bother and excitement about five patients. Nothing in working order and scarcely anything to work with. Major Le Bel is difficult and not a good dresser. I set fire to the ward with an alcohol lamp which won't boil water. No jugs to keep solutions in.

WEDNESDAY, JUNE 2

Such a hot day. Four of our patients sent out. All so glad to get on their way to England. McFadyn, a Glasgow man, left. Our staff were invited to tea at No. 2 Stationary Hospital at La Touquet and quite a few went. My feet are sore so I spent my hours off lying down. Louise McGreer, Clare, and I sat out on the beach this evening.

THURSDAY, JUNE 3

Such a long casualty list today with a great many Canadians. Clare was so glad to hear from her brother Gerald who is at the firing line. We walked up through the poppies which grow in the fields like daisies and buttercups at home. Then on to Étaples to buy cigarettes for Gerald. I got such nice postcards too. Typical of village life in Étaples.

FRIDAY, JUNE 4

Eighty-eight patients. Clare called up last night to help out in receiving patients. She was called at 10 p.m. and the ambulance train did not arrive till 2:30. Such poor management. One couldn't fancy anything worse than the management staff here in every way. A disgrace to Canada. The Matron absolutely useless and not even ladylike, the doctors are such a poor class of men.

SATURDAY, JUNE 5

Another day over. All our men are splendid and some so badly cut up. Grace, Clare, and I walked to Étaples after tea. Bought biscuits and butter for a sleep-in breakfast. Such a lovely day but the country needs rain. Étaples particularly dirty tonight and the number of begging children particularly large. If Canadians knew the manner of the in-charge people they are paying here, they would never stand for it. Col. MacLaren,[28] the O.C. from St. John, is like a man in his dotage and Matron Nesbit is surely quite a bit "off." It is a joke till patients are involved.

SUNDAY, JUNE 6

Gray,[29] McGreer, Clare, and I had breakfast in our hut. Went on duty at 1:30 p.m. to find them evacuating patients. A sacred concert at 7:30 p.m. in our unit's hut with men and patients able to come. Such nice hymn singing. (Officers particularly requested not to attend.) An ambulance van arrived at 9 p.m. Clare up again. 118 patients admitted.

MONDAY, JUNE 7

Such terrible wounds among these patients and such nice men. One boy in our ward is just 20 years old, loses a leg and he is so patient. We had a terrible day. Tate and I discouraged and so tired and it is so unnecessary. Just bad management through and through. The comfort of the patients seems to be the last consideration. It makes one heartsick. No mail again today.

TUESDAY, JUNE 8

A very hot day and another hard, unsatisfactory day for us all. Everybody is disgusted. To think our brothers may someday be brought to this place and to think that it is NOT Canadian. The men are splendid, and some of our orderlies are good and others not so good. Patterson first class. Brunett second. An officer's funeral attended by our officers today. Such a good joke about the raincoat—Col. McLaren.

WEDNESDAY, JUNE 9

The worst day of all. Poor Brown nearly killed in his dressing. I never saw such butchery. Cremin will lose his leg I know. Le Bel[30] is very hard to work with and the Matron simply impossible. We really think a protest or report should be made in some quarters. She is surely batty.

THURSDAY, JUNE 10

A rainy morning and a beautiful afternoon. We evacuated seventeen patients this a.m. in our wards. Another ambulance train in last night, but our ward was filled up so it did not affect us. Cremin to O.R. this a.m. and had his leg amputated. Poor fellow. A bad hand going over this p.m. My half day. Clare and I walked to Paris Plage in p.m., had supper and bought some lovely French lace & embroidery. Such a rest from this atmosphere to have a meal out.

FRIDAY, JUNE 11

A cool day. No receiving last night. "C" ward is peaceful. Cremin is fine and Brown improving every day. I went the rounds trying to add to our ward equipment. Hard work. Saw Capt. Losier today. He hasn't heard from home either. Got a cheque book last night and a cheque for expenses from Montreal to Quebec. Clare and I go exploring after supper, looking for old Roman camp sites. A lovely tramp.

SATURDAY, JUNE 12

Saw three Canadians in Ward L, one of them a Montreal man, Dalhman of Goodwins[31] Smallwares dept. "Under the clock," he said. Clare and I went for a walk along lower Boulogne road till dark. My feet are pretty sore.

SUNDAY, JUNE 13

Another lovely day. Clare and I had such a lovely tramp after duty. We crossed the upper Boulogne road and away back beyond the dunes to splendid, extensive farming. Fields of heavy red clover (new to me) and so many more mares (with foals) tethered by the front foot, horses mostly white. Back home by the same route down the terraced hills and through the pine strip.

MONDAY, JUNE 14

Half day. Went to Paris Plage, then by motor to Montreuil. Such fine roads and beautiful country along the bank of the River Canache, which is just a meadow brook. On through quaint little red-roofed villages along the winding white road, till we came in sight of the old walled town, which has withstood many a siege. Visited for a moment an old church and chapel or Hotel Dieu and bought some PCs [postcards]. A lovely afternoon.

TUESDAY, JUNE 15

An ambulance train in at 5:30 p.m. About fifty patients received here. Not very busy in our ward. Stayed at home and wrote letters in the evening.

WEDNESDAY, JUNE 16

Another ambulance train and fifty patients added to our hospital.

THURSDAY, JUNE 17

180 patients in tonight. Poor lads and some terrible wounds.

FRIDAY, JUNE 18

After supper Clare and I walked to lower Boulogne road, three miles to Camiers where it is rumoured that the McGill Unit is to locate. Camiers is most picturesque, not nearly so dirty as Étaples, and I hear the bathing is good and the shore only a couple of miles away.

SATURDAY, JUNE 19

Col. Birkett's[32] party has arrived at Camiers. A convoy of patients arrived early this a.m. Terrible cases. Kerr, a Highland lad, has practically his face blown away and his body is untouched. It is too cruel. They are all so sick of the war and so glad to be where the gun firing cannot be heard.

SUNDAY, JUNE 20

Walked this p.m. with Clare and Jessie Sedgewick[33] by upper Boulogne road to Camiers, around about seven miles at least. Through farming districts along the hard white Roman road, which winds in and out on the sides of the hills. Got a jug of country wine from a farm house and lunched nearby on the top of a chalk cliff, just above Camiers. The usual farmhouse with its dirty pond with pigs, hens, ducks, etc. Came home in McGill ambulance.

MONDAY, JUNE 21

Went tonight to the rose garden in Étaples (discovered by Clare before). Such a sweet little French woman whose husband is a prisoner. The roses are still beautiful and such an abundance of peonies and sweet peas, also zinnias and delphiniums and Canterbury bells. I bought some seed to send to Mama. Also bought a green vase. There were beautiful large ones too, but impossible to carry.

TUESDAY, JUNE 22

A beautiful day. Half day and Clare and I went to Paris Plage, had our hair washed, then got the motor to go to Hardelot Castle. Such a pretty drive through Camiers, Dannes, Neufchâtel, and Hardelot village. The Lodge is a pretty stone cottage with ivy walls and a lovely garden. The Chateau built in 811 has been rebuilt, but the walls, strengthened by five towers (four of which remain) are as they were. The moat is filled up. Ivy is everywhere and very fine. Dungeons and prisons very well. Chateau being fitted for convalescent hospital.

WEDNESDAY, JUNE 23

Worked hard all day.

THURSDAY, JUNE 24

A usual day. In the evening Clare and I walked down to the Cemetery. Such a pathetic row of small double crosses. One or two Canadians among them. Everything arranged in order and with dignity. My feet are pretty sore.

FRIDAY, JUNE 25

Went to Étaples after supper with Clare. Got to the church for 8 o'clock service. I love to see the old women with their quaint gowns and clean white caps. Saw some beautiful children there. Clare read *Peeps in Picardy*[34] all the way home. (Daylight here till 9 o'clock.) We are certainly having lovely weather, with cool evenings and cold nights.

SATURDAY, JUNE 26

Got off for last hours today and went to Paris Plage with Clare, Giffin,[35] and Miss Steele.[36] Bought a little imitation Copenhagen pin tray. Had tea at the "Chat Bleu" and got home in time for a concert given by English entertainers in our mess tent. Very good and enjoyed so much by the patients who were able to attend. Raining a little this evening. Major Lebel transferred to another ward and we draw Col. Simpson (Winnipeg). He seems very nice and altogether we are pleased.

SUNDAY, JUNE 27

Slept in—such a treat. Spent the morning cleaning up and doing laundry (which I hate). Wrote to Kelchain.

MONDAY, JUNE 28

No convoys from the front recently, and the hospital is emptying gradually. Brown and Cremin put on evacuation list today. This has been a cold and rainy day. Went for a run among the dunes to get warm before going to bed.

TUESDAY, JUNE 29

A convoy of eighty-one patients in last night before midnight, and afterwards an army service corps unloaded all night long and most of today. A Princess Victoria party gave a concert this afternoon in the St. John Ambulance hut for the patients and one in the evening in the Y.M.C.A. hut. We attended. Feeling pretty tired these days.

WEDNESDAY JUNE 30

Another convoy last night. 130 patients. Some bad cases. Mr. Ullock[37] still in and doing well. Going to bed early.

As Ruth's time at No. 1 CGH continues, so too does her recording of pronouncements from the matron in charge. These reflect a matron struggling to exert control and to enforce discipline. Ruth adds her own commentary to each entry. Informing the matron of the commanding officer's upcoming rounds is deemed impossible given the brevity of his visits. As for submission of a daily "complaints list," Ruth thinks that the one from Ward C is lengthy enough to be a requisition slip! On a more serious note is the matron's warning about where tea is not to be served. The CAMC has strict rules and is most paternalistic when it comes to the mixing of the sexes. The all male officer staff have their own area in which to socialize as do the nurses. Males and females are permitted to mix only in designated, supervised spaces. Consequently, the nurses are not to entertain any males, even brothers, for tea in their huts, which are also their bedrooms. The designated anteroom is the only proper place for tea at tea time. As for the last entry concerning the bathing of patients, Ruth no doubt includes it for two reasons. First, with the admission of 81 and 130 patients the previous two nights, the difficulty of bathing each man immediately should be clear to all, matron included. Second, the apparent haste with which the matron writes her note is evident when she appears to be ordering that the night nurses "are to bathe and to see that their patients are bathed" too. Such an error in drafting the order no doubt brought a smile to Ruth's face.

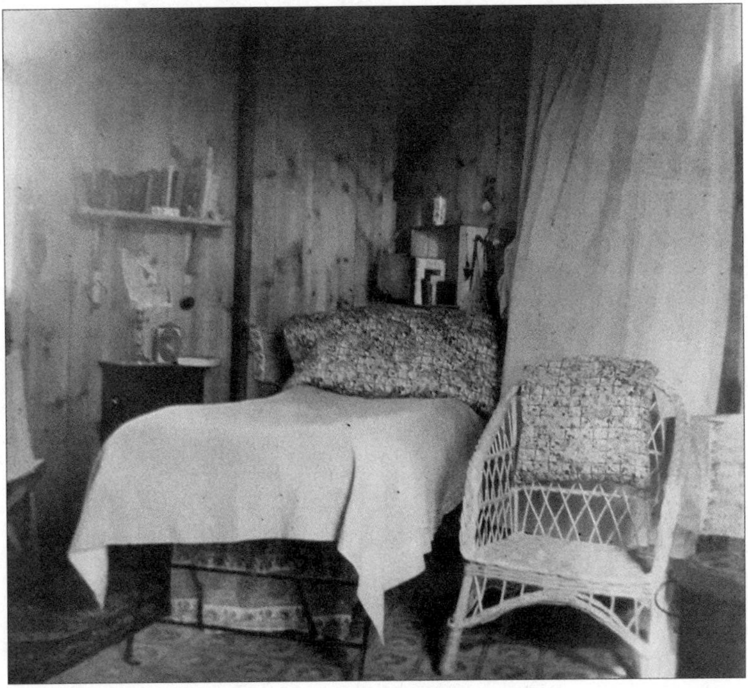

Ruth's living quarters in France–her half of the hut.

NOTICE: When the O.C. is making rounds will the sisters in charge please notify the Matron.

(O.C. Rounds last quite all of two minutes.)

NOTICE: Complaint list or No Complaint list is to be sent each evening to Matron's office.

(Much good it does to complain. The Sisters in C begin to look like a requisition slip.)

The Sisters are please to remember that the very commonest conventional instincts, in every country, forbid that men are to be entertained in bedrooms which at the present time are their huts. No sisters are to go to their huts, or either serve tea there, or dispense it there at that hour (tea hour). Any visitors they may have are to come to the ante room. The only hour at which the Sisters may have tea in their huts is at bed time if they make it themselves.

Any infringement of these rules will carry its own punishment.

Will the thief who took a bottle of glycerin belonging to the Matron from this room replace it.

V. C. Nesbit

WARD POSTER:

When patients are admitted during the hours when the night nursing sisters are on duty they are to bathe and to see that their patients are bathed, each and every patient. No order verbal or otherwise has ever been given by the matron to whom alone the sisters are directly responsible that the patients are not to be bathed on admittance. This is done in all civil hospitals and also in all military hospitals.

June 29th, V. C. Nesbit, Matron

On July 12, Ruth switches tents and moves in with two other nurses who are also starting night duty. Ruth's friction with those in authority at No. 1 CGH reaches its climax on July 22 when she gets a "call down" from the Officer Commanding (O.C.). Three days previous she and Nursing Sister Stevens were called "untrained" and "fishwives" by Matron Nesbit. It is no wonder Ruth wants to leave as soon as possible with the other nurses for No. 3 CGH being erected at Camiers. Ironically, she is not transferred to Camiers until the twenty-fourth, but once moved, she and other nurses make a point of visiting the remaining women of the McGill Unit still stranded at No. 1. Once relocated, Ruth is not very busy, for the hospital is still in the process of being erected. This allows time for exploring as well as swimming at a local beach. After permission is obtained,[38] *the most significant development of the month is the rental of a bicycle. Ruth and her best friend, Clare Gass, now have the means to explore the local countryside beyond walking distance. As the diary makes clear, they do so with zeal. Their thirty-mile round trip on July 29 is but a taste of the exploration they will undertake.*[39]

THURSDAY, JULY 1

Half day. McGriffin, Clare, and I went to Boulogne by the 2 p.m. train and returned by the 8:30 train. Bought a pair of shoes and some stockings and a fountain pen with a cute little elephant head clip (paid 21 francs). Boulogne seems much gayer than when we were there. Had such a nice dinner at the Folkstone Hotel. Such numbers of officers doing nothing.

FRIDAY, JULY 2

A long hard day. Take off a half day and so much work in the ward. Dressings all day. Six cases in last night—three of them bad head cases. Tired and aching all over tonight. No hours off.

SATURDAY, JULY 3

A better day today. Three of us on. Another convoy in last night but our ward not receiving. Brown, Cremen, Price, and two others got off at last this a.m. So glad to see them go. They are so anxious to get to England. Four head cases to O.R. I hope they come out well. Col. Simpson is so particular about them.

SUNDAY, JULY 4

A frightfully hot day. Vomiting all day, not a bit pleasant but all the girls are so nice. Quite fit for duty tomorrow, but posted for night duty tomorrow night. Jean Bell[40] sent to C for the day.

MONDAY, JULY 5

On duty this a.m. after all. Slept in the p.m. somewhat. Don't feel any too good yet. But glad to get to work again. Am going to L, Miss Bliss' ward,[41] also Gray's and Mrs. Archibald's. A misty day but good for sleeping after yesterday. Head cases in C alright yet. Wrote Beatrice A. and Jean and Madge.[42] No letter from home yet.

TUESDAY, JULY 6

An easy night in comparison to the days on C. A convoy in, but L not receiving.

WEDNESDAY, JULY 7

Wrote Ray and Len[43] last night. An easy night. Convoy in again. 100 patients admitted. L not receiving.

THURSDAY, JULY 8

A frightful blowy night. A convoy last night. 180 patients and 140 evacuated this a.m. There must be lots doing at the front these days. Letters from Ray, Helen L.,[44] Mrs. Young, Alice K., and Mrs. Sutherland. Such a treat. Wrote poor Mrs. Orr who has lost her father. Also Mrs. Young. She is a dear to write to me as she does.

FRIDAY, JULY 9

A beautiful morning. Went for a stroll with Fortesque and secured some lovely flowers for our tent. Such sweet little pink peas and morning glories. Had a busy night—two convoys, six patients each time. Not so interesting as surgical but less harrowing. Slept in a.m. but wide awake all p.m.

SATURDAY, JULY 10

Slept all day. Clare went to Paris Plage and bargained for bicycles for $10 a month. We will go in Monday for them if I feel equal to it. Another easy night.

SUNDAY, JULY 11

Such a good sleep but such a waste of beautiful days when one is on night duty. One gets wonderful sun risings though, and the birds begin their singing at 2:30 when day begins to break.

MONDAY, JULY 12

A convoy last night—seventeen received in L, two Canadians. Clare and I went to Paris Plage, brought our bicycles home. I moved over the hill this a.m. in with Pidgeon and Sewell.[45] Three in a hut now, and this place is so sandy and dusty and noisy.

TUESDAY, JULY 13

Was so tired and sleepy last night and sick at my stomach. Slept all day and could hardly persuade myself to get up for duty. Another convoy last night.

WEDNESDAY, JULY 14

Slept like a top all day. Nothing exciting at night except a terrific rainstorm with heavy wind. Not a leak in our tent. Letter from Len.

THURSDAY, JULY 15

Letters from Dickie and Effie Brown and papers from Watling. Slept all day and feel so much better tonight. Hope to go for a bicycle ride in the morning. Wrote Effie.

FRIDAY, JULY 16

Wrote Len last night. How I dread the day he leaves Canada, and he is looking forward to it naturally. Miss Lindsay[46] and I rode to Étaples to market and bought some cherries. I love market day in Étaples. There is such a crowd of people and their fruit and vegetables are very good. Raining again this evening. Papers from home here for Sunday.

SATURDAY, JULY 17

A wild stormy night. A good test for the tent, which held firm. Too noisy for much sleep today. Col. Birkett has asked us for us and we may go tomorrow or Monday. Matron McLatchey here for Sunday.

Just before leaving No. 1 CGH, Ruth records one last entry from its matron:

Sister MacIntosh, why haven't you sent in your Sunday hours as usual yesterday? Sisters who do not send in her hours should go without them as punishment.

No. 2 A hundred apologies but some thief took it, for I did not see the envelope.

Yours, V. C. Nesbit

SUNDAY, JULY 18

My birthday. Clare and I went for such a lovely ride this a.m. Up through the country on the upper Boulogne road. Oh, it is so beautiful. Clare gave me one of her little jugs for my birthday and I love it very much. No definite word of our leaving. Will be sorry to leave my nice men in L.

MONDAY, JULY 19

Taken off duty at 10:30 p.m. Handed my nice ward over to a French Canadian nurse. On coming to bed [Matron] Violet [Nesbitt] appeared in nightgown to inform Stevie and I that we were more like a couple of untrained nurses. She also told Stewart[47] we were like a gang of fishwives. Not posted for a ward and off duty all day. Most of the girls left for McGill in the afternoon. Pidgeon on duty in L. Sewell and I do nothing all day.

TUESDAY, JULY 20

Posted for support tent. There for half an hour, then sent to H to special a pneumonia case. Had my half day after first being told that supply nurses never have half days. Lill and Clare came and we all went to Paris Plage and had tea at the Chat Bleu. Clare and I wheeled home, the rest going in the swim machine. Arrived at No. 1 to find more girls going to No. 3. Just seven of us left.

WEDNESDAY, JULY 21

Posted for Ward L, such luck. Gray and Roberts and McMillian and me. I kept out of sight during rounds and was off from 11–2. A number of girls not posted at all. Rainy in p.m. so no bicycle rides.

THURSDAY, JULY 22

In ward L. Hours off 1–4 and it rained the entire time. Got two letters from Ray enclosing one from Irene telling about the wedding to be. Got a "call down" from the O.C. for spoiling the patients and for talking back. He certainly is a disgrace to Canada and to Saint John particularly. He reported ward L to Violet who in turn came to us. No sentimentally inclined sisters to be placed there.

FRIDAY, JULY 23

On duty in L as usual. Had afternoon hours and went off at 3 p.m. to find my name posted with Stephens and Carpenter[48] to go down to No. 3. Also found my trunk packed by Buchanan, which made me <u>furious</u>. Such are the ways of No. 1.

SATURDAY, JULY 24

It is lovely here and I like the tents equally as well as the huts. Lill and Tina[49] went to Paris Plage by bus. Clare and I following on our wheels. Had a nice dinner at the hotel, then shopped. Dickie and I ordering cretonne[50] and are buying a table, mat, etc. Coming home Clare and I stopped off at No. 1 and visited Hollie Carmen[51] who is very miserable and unhappy with a bad headache. I do wish they were all down with us.

SUNDAY, JULY 25

Wrote home. Green envelope.[52] Service at 10:30. Captain Shatford our clergyman here. After lunch we were ordered to be ready for Field Marshall French to inspect us, but he failed to appear. Service at 6 p.m. and in the evening Clare, Lill, Tina, Miss Woods, and I went for a walk toward Dannes. Gathering children as we went till there were twenty-eight in our train. Dickie was very much amused.

MONDAY, JULY 26

A beautiful day. Went bathing in the morning. The tide very high and the water clear green. In the afternoon Clare and I bicycled to Neufchâtel—such a very pretty village with some fine country homes. Clare and I compose a flower committee, and it is quite a problem as wild flowers are scarce just now. After supper Shephie and I wheeled to No. 1 and saw Tate and Sallie Gray, all longing to be here. Letter from Dolman.[53]

TUESDAY, JULY 27

Posted for duty at 9 a.m. in a medical hut No. K3 with Miss Bliss, also De Core,[54] Whitney,[55] and T. Macdonald. Nothing much to do as Ward is not stocked. Went bicycling back country after tea as usual going far afield and had to rush back to be just a little late for supper.

WEDNESDAY, JULY 28

Went bathing in a.m. Tide very rough. Such a wind blowing. The piano arrived this afternoon so we have lots of music. On duty in p.m. Rather busy taking stock in K and L; 1 and 2.

THURSDAY, JULY 29

On duty in a.m. Doing little duties in K, not making beds up yet. In p.m. (sick with headache and all), Clare and I went touring to Boulogne via Dannes and Neufchâtel. There on towards Desvres, turning off to our left to visit a little church at Wirwignes built by a curé with his own hands. Quite a wonderful monument and well worth another visit. Home by Tamer and Montreuil roads through Frencq, getting home at 10:10 coming down the hill. A very wonderful afternoon. Will go to Desvres another afternoon.

FRIDAY, JULY 30

Posted for L2 and in charge. Miss Forgey[56] and Miss Harrison[57] for staff sisters. Would far sooner be in K2 with Miss Bliss. Got our beds in order and dishes marked. Dickie and Watling on duty in p.m. Went to the station for our cretonne, which will be very pretty. Dickie and I wheeled to No. 1 in the evening. Saw Capt. Losier. I spoke to him about Mrs. Orr. Brought my pillow home and we arrived in our lines at 9:30.

SATURDAY, JULY 31

On duty in a.m. Made up the beds and sent in requisitions. After supper Mrs. Austin and I took the bus up to No. 1 and walked back. Saw Miss MacDonald from Chatham,[58] also Miss Cummings. No home letters yet.

Having arrived at No. 3 CGH, Ruth settles into a routine of work. On August 7, she, Clare, and Dickie are all detailed to night shift duty in their respective wards. Despite working all night they still have the energy to go places and do things in the morning before they go to bed. These morning activities include both walks and bicycle rides. After one of these excursions, Clare comments in her diary, "Really I know no two other women who have as much endurance as Ruth & I. We both had a fairly busy night & though we did not get home til one o'clock we were not nearly so tired as we were entitled to be."[59] *But all is not work and excursions, for there are baseball games to watch–an activity at which the McGill Unit's men seem to excel if the number of times they defeat the American Harvard Unit's team is any indication. There are also travelling entertainers, like the Princess Victoria Concert Party, who perform in the local YMCA tent. These travelling acts from England range in character from highbrow to popular to vaudevillian and are well received by both the hospital staff and the recovering soldiers.*

SUNDAY, AUGUST 1

On duty in a.m. Did not go into service. After lunch Louise McGreer and Lill and I went up the hill to write letters and had such a nice time. Saw some clever handling of a flock of sheep in the valley by a couple of shepherds and dogs. After supper Watling, Lill, and I went to No. 1 by bus and walked home. Wrote home but no mail for me today.

MONDAY, AUGUST 2

Sports day but the p.m. so rainy that a bad game between No. 1 and No. 3 was left unfinished with a heavy score for McGill. A.D.M.S.[60] is to make rounds and so sports postponed. Concert in the YMCA in the evening by Victoria party. Very good and much appreciated by patients. Very heavy rain in evening. Matron Nesbitt here for tea and ballgame.

TUESDAY, AUGUST 3

Sports came off this p.m. The "darn Canadians" walking off with everything with exception of officers tug of war. Dickie won seventy-five yard race, and Watling won in thread and needle race. Got a pail and shovel. Prizes given out by M. Darge in YMCA after another concert given by same party. We girls cheered everything. Letter from Len who is still in Sussex. Lovely letter from home.

WEDNESDAY, AUGUST 4

Off for the day. Clare and I went to Paris Plage, going to Étaples by Frencq and other villages. Lovely country everywhere. Had lunch in Paris Plage and I bought some finery to send to Irene. A nightgown and wee pincushion. Both of us came home without a pence. Called at No. 1 and watched the boys at baseball. Reached here in time for War Anniversary service.

THURSDAY, AUGUST 5

Wrote Irene and sent box and cards to H. On duty in a.m. Sewed cretonne for a trunk cover and hung around the ward and mess tent in turn to be looked at by General Hughes[61] whom I did not see after all. Such a fuss over these fellows. Dickie and I went for a wheel after tea to Dannes and from there by a new road to the sea. Saw where a huge hotel was ruined, partly washed away by the tide five years ago.

FRIDAY, AUGUST 6

On duty in a.m. in "A," Miss McLeod[62] in charge. Another ward to equip. Clare, Lill, Tena, and I went to Boulogne after lunch and I got new fountain pen, also rain hats to send to the girls. We had quite a nice afternoon and ride both ways. Boulogne is a much larger city than I thought. The approaches are all barred up with trucks. It isn't easy to get there now without a proper pass.

SATURDAY, AUGUST 7

Dickie and I finished fixing up our hut this morning and we feel very grand. On duty in p.m. Baseball game between Harvard and McGill—7 to 4 in favour of McGill. They said it was a grand game. A convoy in at 8:30 p.m. Lill, Clare, and I are on night duty. "A" ward now opened and I am in Observation tent. Three patients with excuses.

SUNDAY, AUGUST 8

Slept all day and off duty tonight as my patients were transferred to "K."

MONDAY, AUGUST 9

On duty in p.m. Made beds. Called up for convoy at nine but decided "A" was not ready so I helped Dickie receive. Went to bed at 5 a.m.

TUESDAY, AUGUST 10

A convoy in at 8 a.m. and "A" received twelve patients. Very inconvenient without screens or bedside tables. They have given me such a nice student as orderly, LeBel.[63] Dickie worked with him on *Metagama* and liked him so much.

WEDNESDAY, AUGUST 11

On duty as usual.

THURSDAY, AUGUST 12

Clare, Miss Steele, and I went wheeling after breakfast. Up over the hill and out the Neufchâtel roads. A lovely ride, got wet coming home, but the rain cleared off as we came into camp.

FRIDAY, AUGUST 13

A quiet night.

SATURDAY, AUGUST 14

Clare, Miss Steel, and I wheeled to Paris Plage after breakfast to pay our rental. A nice ride but it did not pay. One o'clock before I got to bed. Such a letter treat, Ray, Winnie, Mrs. Sutherland, and Madge heard from and a "World"[64] from home.

SUNDAY, AUGUST 15

No entry

MONDAY, AUGUST 16

No entry

TUESDAY, AUGUST 17

A small convoy this evening.

WEDNESDAY, AUGUST 18

A quiet night. The day not so quiet.

THURSDAY, AUGUST 19

Wrote Helen L. and sent cards to Greig. Everything goes as usual. Another small convoy. Patients mostly from other hospitals.

FRIDAY, AUGUST 20

After waiting half an hour for the car as promised us, we were informed that the O.C. had taken it so our trip was off. We went to bed mad and spent a miserable sleepless day. Sent P.C. to Rae L.

SATURDAY, AUGUST 21

Went to bed early and slept better than usual. Clare and Miss Steele went to Paris Plage. Got up in time for the last of a baseball match. Harvard and McGill. Letters from Miss Richardson and Mrs. Dunn tonight. Clare and Lill and I walked through the village and distributed sweets instead of pennies.

SUNDAY, AUGUST 22

No entry

MONDAY, AUGUST 23

A small convoy in last night. We took two "walk-ins."[65]

TUESDAY, AUGUST 24

Clare and I wheeled to Paris Plage to get Clare's glasses. Her wheel went just as we started and it was with difficulty that we got to the village. The Bicycle man was away in Paris so we had to take the car home, waiting for the bus about fifteen minutes. Found Gray at Étaples.

TUESDAY, AUGUST 25

Another convoy last night. Five patients coming to us. One sick man. I felt worried about him this a.m.

WEDNESDAY, AUGUST 26

A quiet night. Our sick man seems better. Clare and I went to Paris Plage. Walked to Étaples and wait[ed] till 11:10 for the car. Got home at one o'clock. We called at the cemetery for a moment to locate Dunn's grave. A really hot day, too hot for wheeling. Not much sleep today.

THURSDAY, AUGUST 27

Lill, Clare, and I went bathing this a.m. and found the tide pretty far out and were nearly eaten by the sea bugs or something of that species. Late getting to bed as usual. A hot noisy night. A convoy last night. We received three.

FRIDAY, AUGUST 28

A quiet night. Went to bed immediately after breakfast. A baseball match this afternoon. Officers and men. Men won of course.

SATURDAY, AUGUST 29

Slept all day.

SUNDAY, AUGUST 30

Convoy expected tonight.

MONDAY, AUGUST 31

Zeppelin raid scare today but nothing happened.

September begins, not unusually, with rain. The soil on which the tent hospital at Camiers is pitched turns into fields of sticky mud. Ruth, like the soldiers, is to have her share of the mud of France. Still, despite the frequent rain, Ruth and Clare continue to explore on their bicycles. Their trip on September 7 covers forty kilometres each way! Ruth's diary bears testimony to another aspect of life at No. 3 CGH–the frequency of visits by dignitaries. Sir William Osler, McGill's famous and well-connected unofficial patron in England, was accompanied on September 10 by Canadian nursing Matron-in-Chief Margaret MacDonald and Lady Perley. Both Osler and MacDonald have relatives serving in No. 3 CGH. On September 20, the Queen of Portugal visits, and the next day the Director General of Canadian Overseas Medical Services, General G. C. Jones, and British Surgeon General Sir George Makins make an appearance. These visitors, although an inconvenience for the nurses who have to have their wards spic and span for the occasion, actually serve a practical purpose. The dignitaries cheer the patients, and their comments of approval concerning the McGill Unit are carefully recorded and duly publicized. These mutual admiration events both serve to bolster the reputation of McGill's hospital and help to ensure the steady flow of support from the home front.

Finally, at month's end, word to increase bed capacity by five hundred and the clearing out of patients on September 25 and 26 are foreboding omens–the waves of newly wounded commence the very next day. The "push," the British Battle of Loos, would continue into October. The wounded will continue to come.

TUESDAY, SEPTEMBER 1

Such a storm of wind and rain today from the south, the fulfillment of the early morning sky. Days are short now and the sun much later in the morning showing above the hills.

WEDNESDAY, SEPTEMBER 2

Clare and I wheeled to Paris Plage in spite of the dark clouds and got back before it rained. Saw such a quaint scene in Étaples on our way. A sailor man returning and greeting the village men, women, and children with kisses on both cheeks. Étaples always treating us to some new scene.

THURSDAY, SEPTEMBER 3

Such a downpour of rain all night and very cold and damp. It continued all day with the result that the whole camp is very dirty. The clay soil is so sticky when wet.

FRIDAY, SEPTEMBER 4

It rained torrents all last night and the greater part of today. Rumours about that we are to be moved away from here before too long.

SUNDAY, SEPTEMBER 5

Went this a.m. through Neufchâtel and around by the Veterinary camp to Hardelot Plage. Such a beautiful beach with pretty boulevard and terrace. An ideal summer resort—unspoiled. There is a hospital here for the Hindus. Returning past the lake and golf links to the Chateau and home by the Boulogne Road. Went right to bed and slept like a top. Such a lovely morning ride. I'll not forget it.

MONDAY, SEPTEMBER 6

Clare and I went to Étaples after breakfast to buy eats. A nice ride and saw a donkey with panniers and a girl in charge. Such a perfect subject for a snap. Arrived home by noon.

TUESDAY, SEPTEMBER 7

A convoy last night, which gave us a busy night. Our last night and I'm sorry after all my wishing to be off. Lapp[66] is such a splendid boy. He has been very nice to me, and I'm sorry to leave the patients. They are so ill and I am used to them. I am to go to "E" I believe. Lapp and I very late getting our work done. Don't know what happened to us. <u>A perfect day</u>. Clare and I started after breakfast, went to Étaples, and then back to Touquet through Cucq and Merlimont past a huge Army Service Camp along a level road. Sometimes in the dunes but mostly through low lying meadow and to Berck. Got past 4 sentries by smiles and Clare's French, then on to Rue, which is

Clare's camera–the source of most of the photos in this book.

a lovely town. Had lunch and chatted with a boy lately come there from near the Belgium border. After lunch we visited the Chapelle du Saint-Esprit, the interior of which is highly decorated and too distinctly French in some ways. The exterior is very beautiful with its cluster of figures. These figures suffered during the Revolution. Some are utterly destroyed, others are headless. We left the town with regret, but time was short and the return ride long. On our return to Berck we went on to Berck Plage, which is a large, up-to-date watering place with excellent shopping. Back past new sentries with old questions about passes, which we did not have. The return ride was lovely but long. We arrived in Camp in early time for late dinner, tired and sleepy, but it was such a perfect, happy day. Clare and I do have good times.

WEDNESDAY, SEPTEMBER 8

Duty again. Off at 4:30.

THURSDAY, SEPTEMBER 9

On duty in "E" with Miss MacIntosh. A quiet ward and I find myself quite lonely for Ward A. I always hate changes. Off duty from 10 a.m.–3 p.m. It seems a lot of time to oneself after night hours, and it is good to have a night's sleep again. Went bathing before lunch and Lill lost her teeth, was scared out of my wits for a moment till she found them again.

FRIDAY, SEPTEMBER 10

My half day and I do nothing. Clare and I went bathing after lunch and found the tide very far out and sea lice numerous. A beautiful day but too windy for bicycling. A bridge party on tonight in Sir William's honor. Matron-in-Chief MacDonald and Lady Perley also here visiting. McGill is getting too much attention. The 6th year men are leaving us I fear for a return to school.

SATURDAY, SEPTEMBER 11

No entry

SUNDAY, SEPTEMBER 12

No entry

MONDAY, SEPTEMBER 13

No entry

TUESDAY, SEPTEMBER 14

Princess Louise visited us today, going through the O.R. and a few of the wards. Clare and I wheeled to Paris Plage to pay our rent, and the party, including our friend the A.D.M.S., passed us. We came home in thirty minutes for last supper.

WEDNESDAY, SEPTEMBER 15

No entry

THURSDAY, SEPTEMBER 16

Convoy of 180 last night. Clare and I took our long planned trip to Desvres in spite of the threatening weather. It was a happy afternoon. We bought some Desvres pottery, Clare a vase and I a jug. We passed through Samer both ways but took new roads, going through a beautiful wood before joining the Montreuil road. Came home through Dannes. No letters yet.

FRIDAY, SEPTEMBER 17

Hours off, 1–4 p.m. Helped cut bread and butter and darned Clare's stockings while she read to me. Went to Col. McCrae's lecture in the evening.[67] McConnell and Stewart and

Dorothy Cotton[68] back from leave today and little Tate, Miss Steele, and Miss Archibald leave. Ten minutes after they got off, orders came to cancel all leave given. More channel trouble.

SATURDAY, SEPTEMBER 18

Wakened with a queer headache and Miss MacIntosh insisted on my going off. Went back on duty at 3 p.m. and finished up the day's work. I am to change to another ward in the morning, I hear. Perhaps I will get settled after a bit. Letters from Mama and Ray and Len and one from Mrs. Dunn. Mama had a lovely trip to Truro. I am so glad for her. Startling news for Montreal of Ida Geegan's death at the M.G.H. No particulars. I fancy Lockhart Gall is the medium through which news came. Joint letter from Mr. and Mrs. Grey, too.

SUNDAY, SEPTEMBER 19

No entry

MONDAY, SEPTEMBER 20

The ex-queen of Portugal honoured us today going to a few of the wards.

TUESDAY, SEPTEMBER 21

Gen. Jones and Sir Geo. Markham the Surgeon General paid us a visit today. We are very gay.

WEDNESDAY, SEPTEMBER 22

Half day, our plan for Boulogne knocked out by the Matron. After giving necessary attention to two punctures we went to Montreuil and had a lovely afternoon going by Neuville and returning from the other side of the city to Beutin. We had tea at the Hotel France in the courtyard. Got home for a second dinner and went to Y.M.C.A. concert, which was horrid.

THURSDAY, SEPTEMBER 23

No entry

FRIDAY, SEPTEMBER 24

No entry

SATURDAY, SEPTEMBER 25

"Worlds" from home tonight. White and Ruby Graham and Seaborne R. and Chisholm went to an English Hospital for a few days. Our hospital increased its capacity by 500 beds. Church tent and sergeant's mess both filled with beds.

SUNDAY, SEPTEMBER 26

Every possible patient evacuated for Hospital Ship. Cases otherwise for base details got with Blighty. Clare and I walked to Dannes to the church and gave sweets to the kiddies. Poor Clare is worried about the boys. Tate, Miss Steele, and Miss Archibald back from leave tonight. Letter from Irene. Service in our ante tents.

MONDAY, SEPTEMBER 27

A convoy of 220 in last night, terrible cases, so many heads. Three deaths in A and H tent. A great many Gordon Highlanders admitted and tell of their regiment being almost wiped out. Over 500 patients came to camp last night. A rainy day today.

TUESDAY, SEPTEMBER 28

Another convoy last night. More terrible wounds. We are very busy. Another rainy day and very cold. News from the front is very good today. Letter from Ray tonight. Such a nice long one with an account of Helen's wedding.[69]

WEDNESDAY, SEPTEMBER 29

Still another rainy day. The camp is very mucky and slippery. Another convoy tonight. The men are all sick and cold and miserable. News from the front is still very good, but the cost is great.

THURSDAY, SEPTEMBER 30

Another convoy last night. We are all very busy with such enormous dressings. Clare is miserable tonight with a high temperature. Am afraid she is in for grippe. It is a case of eat and sleep and work these days, and we are short with Miss Duncan and Miss Cotton and the girls to the British Hospital gone.

The influx of wounded from the battle of Loos persists into October. By the fourth, Ruth relates that they received one thousand patients in the past week. While such a rush is on, it is impossible for the nurses to perform many of their daily tasks, and so Ruth's comment: wound "dressings, dressings from morning to night." Even as the "push" eases, the war news is not good–the Germans retake trenches won earlier, word of nurse deaths on the Dardanelle front reaches France, and an American nurse at a neighbouring hospital dies of disease. On the seventeenth, Ruth learns that a cousin is wounded and is in a nearby hospital. Kerr Loggie of the 26th Infantry Battalion, who is from Chatham, NB, has a broken arm and bruised back from being buried alive by shell fire, injuries from which he will recover. Ruth visits him and then writes both his mother and her sister providing details and assuring them of his eventual recovery. This incident epitomizes the multifaceted role that Great War nurses find themselves in. They not only treat the wounded and often write the soldiers' families on their behalf, but they have family of their own who become the wounded. In these instances, nurses serve as a two-way conduit for unofficial, first-hand, intimate, unabridged "family" news of their loved ones' true condition.

Finally, October brings much colder weather to France. Ruth mentions their tents being moved to make way for the construction of winter huts and the use of oil-burning stoves in an attempt to stay warm. She also tells of running to keep warm and of longing to kick the ball about as the men do in an effort to generate some warmth. Ball kicking with the boys is not seen as an acceptable female activity.

FRIDAY, OCTOBER 1

Work still keeping ahead of us. I never get the beds made. It's dressings, dressings from morning to night. The weather is still rainy and most of the girls wear their rubber aprons all day. I never take my rubbers off.

SATURDAY, OCTOBER 2

Another rainy, busy day with a large evacuation. Clare still miserable with a temp. She should be off duty.

SUNDAY, OCTOBER 3

Clare off today and the sun is out with us at last. The wards still busy, though our bridal chamber is empty of its grouches, and I got the beds made in proper order and had two hours off.

MONDAY, OCTOBER 4

Another convoy last night. Our hospital received a thousand patients last week. Had regular time off.

TUESDAY, OCTOBER 5

A better day. We are getting straightened out and some stock made up, but our patients are very sick. Four of them on the danger list.

WEDNESDAY, OCTOBER 6

Stevie and I wheeled to Paris Plage. Day off and Clare and I went to Dannes for service, which was a pathetic little affair, just five women there and no priest. News today that Mrs. Jaggard and another nurse in the Dardanelles are dead with dysentery.[70] Col. McKee very ill too.

THURSDAY, OCTOBER 7

Another evacuation this a.m. But our remaining patients are on the danger list. Today's paper says part of the trenches captured last week have been retaken by the Germans.

FRIDAY, OCTOBER 8

Went up on the hills after dinner and read. A cool day, quite a "fall air" but so lovely. Miss MacIntosh goes on night duty and Miss Brand[71] comes to me for head nurse.

SATURDAY, OCTOBER 9

No entry

SUNDAY, OCTOBER 10

Went up the hills with Clare and "Potash and Perlmutter."[72] It's a breezy day—very drafty.

MONDAY, OCTOBER 11

Thanksgiving Day

Very important day. We are given mattresses. Orders are that hospital beds to be reduced to 1,000. Hence the extra mattresses. We carried ours down and have now a regular double bed.

TUESDAY, OCTOBER 12

Bicycled to Neufchâtel with Clare round a lovely little road behind the grounds we admire from the village road. Capt. Shatford leaves today and Capt. Hepburn[73] replaces him. He is a son of Miss Gauvin's old clergyman.

WEDNESDAY, OCTOBER 13

Today's report says that No. 2 Stationary is to go near Boulogne. Two new sisters, Miss Stewart and Miss Lamont, both R.V., take Miss Duncan's and Miss Cotton's places.

THURSDAY, OCTOBER 14

Half day. Clare and I wheeled to Boulogne. A beautiful hot afternoon but a thick mist to wheel through in the evening. Clare bought a Paris doll, about 18 in. in box at back of bicycle. We bought lamps and mine turned out "no good" so will have to return it. Sgt. Williams died today.

FRIDAY, OCTOBER 15

Convoy at 8:30 this a.m. 103 cases so the day goes quickly. Some bad cases, but not as last week.

SATURDAY, OCTOBER 16

Turkey dinner tonight. Our tents are moved over on the rising ground next to No. 18. So our winter quarters may be started.

SUNDAY, OCTOBER 17

Hours off 1–4. Clare and I wheeled back over the hills exploring a new wood, not very satisfactory as we had to get back for dinner. I wrote home. Got a note from Mr. Archibald this evening telling me that Kerr Loggie is a patient in the St. John Ambulance Hospital.

MONDAY, OCTOBER 18

Hours off 4–8. Wheeled up to see Kerr L. He has a fractured arm and a bruised back from being buried but looks well. Wrote Mrs. L. and Rae. Our ward is very idle these days. Miss MacIntosh on night superintendant duty and Miss Stewart in her place.

TUESDAY, OCTOBER 19

A cold bright day. No convoys. Evacuated two patients this a.m. Watling and Lill off for their day and gone to Paris Plage and will call to see Kerr. Clare too gone to P.P. Clare and I went for a run before bedtime to get warmed up, and I started a letter to and a letter from Ray. Feed of chicken in Watling's room.

WEDNESDAY, OCTOBER 20

I had Laura morning hours. D. E. F. moved into G, a staff nurse going with patients of each ward and a "supply" tent started with Clare in charge. Stevie and I are together, thank fortune. Miss Enright in charge with Handcock. Our happy home in E is broken up for good and all, I suppose. Price and Montil and Ross go on fatigue duty.

THURSDAY, OCTOBER 21

Another cold day. Our huts are going steadily up. I feel very strange in "G," but each change makes one feel so. I have last hours and wish I could kick the ball with the boys to keep warm. This morning's mist has cleared away, but it is still very chilly. The stoves ordered came today and our tent feels fairly warm. We are to use oil til the Government tells us to stop.

FRIDAY, OCTOBER 22

Such sad news from the Chicago hospital. Today a sister has died very suddenly.[74] We have not heard for sure of what. Strep C infection is mentioned, but nothing is definite. It will be a sad hospital and many difficult letters to write. Letter from Ray with news of an arrival at Uncle Will's—a son. May and Lewis will be very proud.

SATURDAY, OCTOBER 23

A large convoy this a.m. Not very bad cases. My half day. Extra buses ran to Étaples for Sister Hamilton's funeral, which was at 3 p.m. Clare and I wheeled and joined the sisters going from No. 1 as our girls were in outdoor uniform. The hospital was well represented and the service was well conducted. The procession from the mortuary to grave was pathetic, but the whole scene was very impressive and will not be easily forgotten. Clare and I went on to Paris Plage and I bought a chicken for the boys, also some handkerchiefs for Len for Xmas. Dusk found us still at the Swiss shop and we had left our lamps at home. Clare and Watling helped us eat a pineapple cake in our tent after supper. I have a cold, which is a real nuisance and hard on the hands. Suzanne brought back my uniform, which she has had for four weeks. Not fit to wear. Such are the dress problems.

SUNDAY, OCTOBER 24

A cold day with rain in the afternoon. Hours off 10–3. Cleaned up our tent and wrote home. We have an addition to our ante tent, a local paper "Sunday Observer," origin unknown, a four leafed affair badly typed, with stale war news and original scraps of "life about camp."

MONDAY, OCTOBER 25

Such a furious rain storm last night and all day today. One of E tents ripped straight across and the patients were moved to F. It was very uncomfortable working today. Everything is wet. The patients are so cold. We tramp around in long rubber boots and get chilblains. Several of the tents came down and our pegs are loose or out.

TUESDAY, OCTOBER 26

So glad to wake to a sunny day. It is very cold but the wind is drying things up and the wards are more cheerful. Was off from 3 to 6 o'clock. Clare is reciting at a concert for the convalescent Camp, and Watling and Dickie and Tate have gone with her. Glendenning[75] is singing. We are going to Boulogne tomorrow. Lill, Watling, Clare, Armitage, and I by train. A rainy afternoon.

WEDNESDAY, OCTOBER 27

Went to Boulogne on the 8:40 train and spent the day. Got a photo frame for Len and Laura's picture, and I got underwear. Had such a nice lunch at the Folkstone and I got my hair washed. Capt. Dixon[76] came home with us at 10 p.m. The only day we have had without rain.

THURSDAY, OCTOBER 28

Another rainy day.

FRIDAY, OCTOBER 29

Letters from Len and Ray tonight. Len has no idea when they leave Val Cartier.

SATURDAY, OCTOBER 30

Another rainy day with bright half-hour intervals. Ball game on between No. 22 British and our hospital. Our boys won. Stevie and I wheeled to Étaples in last hours and had our usual fun. Bought nuts and apples and bread and dates and talked French. Got home for second supper.

SUNDAY, OCTOBER 31

Specialized Freeman today. He had another hemorrhage last night but is holding his own today. And is as disagreeable as possible. Off duty from 1:30 to 3 p.m. and tramped over the hills by myself to keep warm.

With November comes more rain, higher winds, colder temperatures, and finally on the sixteenth, snow. The tent hospital at Camiers is condemned as unfit for winter habitation by either patients or staff. Patients are moved on, the wards disassembled, some nurses are temporarily reassigned to other hospitals, and the remainder, like Ruth, stay and wait. Given the horrible weather, waiting is not easy, and under the circumstances, returning their bicycles on the seventeenth is no real hardship. Fortunately, all is not misery. On the first there is a Halloween costume party for officers and nurses, and on the second a similar party, hosted by the nurses, for the NCOs and "other rank" men of the McGill Unit. The men return the favour on the eighteenth. The month also witnesses the birth of the unit newspaper, the McGilliken. *While Ruth thought little of its predecessor, the* Sunday Observer, *she is quite taken by this new production. Receiving no patients means there is more time to go into Boulogne, Paris Plage, or Neufchâtel and enjoy a meal at one of the restaurants. On November twenty-first they learn that they will eventually be moving into an old monastery in Boulogne for winter quarters. However, the site will require significant work before the nurses can take up residence.*

MONDAY, NOVEMBER 1

Our party night. Dickie and I went in sheets and pillowcases and the party was a fair good time. Not enough music but the decorations and eats were fine. I relieved Gillis[77] for an hour. Freeman is cross and none too well. I'm afraid he isn't coming out on top.

TUESDAY, NOVEMBER 2

Such a perfectly splendid party and everyone had such a good time. Our boys are just the nicest in the world. Cooper[78] started the evening as Bluebeard and nearly ended it with a tragedy as she set fire to her beard and only her usual presence of mind saved the situation. I went with only a mask and had the time of my life as nobody recognized me. Price was the dear Duchess and was splendidly gotten up. Dickie went in uniform and Clare as Dr. Hopkins.

WEDNESDAY, NOVEMBER 3

Freeman has been quiet all day but so irritable and hard to manage and looks so white and ill. Major Archibald seems to be quite cheerful, but we are pessimistic. I sat outdoors all afternoon with him and got chilled to the bone. Latest rumour—we are going to Shorncliffe. Wrote Mrs. Freeman.

THURSDAY, NOVEMBER 4

A worrisome day. Freeman had another hemorrhage last night. Had an intravenous this a.m. and a transfusion this p.m. 600cc from Capt. Reford, who must feel the loss. The improvement on Freeman's part was marvelous, but I am afraid it can't be lasting. He is much more agreeable today and I hated leaving him. Mrs. Drake[79] gave a dancing lesson this evening. Clare and I went for a walk and I ordered chicken at the Hotel du Lac.

FRIDAY, NOVEMBER 5

Freeman died this a.m. at 8 and I feel lost and very badly in consequence, but his recovery was almost too much to expect. Off from 10–3 and Miss Hounes came and told me to take the day off as there was little to do. Wrote Mama and Alice and Mrs. Cooper. Got our chickens and bought a cauliflower. Letter from home tonight and paper for Gray. Such a nice snap of Wib[80] in Ray's letter. Carrie has a daughter.

SATURDAY, NOVEMBER 6

Clare and I wheeled to Paris Plage with Miss Steel, and I bought a locket and chain for Ray's birthday. Such a dear old rose enamel one set with chip diamonds. Clare got a hair wash and we had chocolate at the "corner cake shop." Miss Steel ran into a man on our way home—our only excitement. It gets dark so soon now. Ordered a baby dress for May King. *The Sunday Observer* has changed its name to *The McGilliken* and the editing staff is made public. Capt. MacDonald Editor in chief with Bieler, Gallagher, and Jenkins assistants. Our party is well written up with excellent impressions by our dishwasher, Rosie.

SUNDAY, NOVEMBER 7

A very cold night, the ground hard and covered with white frost this a.m. A cold dull day. Slept in and such an unfortunate morning. Dickie's underwear, which hung over the stove, got so smoked up that I had to wash it all over, which took up most of the entire a.m. Went for a short bicycle ride with Clare after lunch down to Neufchâtel. Our rides are now numbered as our wheels go back for good on the 16th. Pte. Billor admitted to G tonight with suspected renal colic. He is one of the sub editors of *The McGilliken.*

MONDAY, NOVEMBER 8

Such a lovely warm day. Off from 3 p.m. Walked on the hills with Bradley[81] till teatime and then waited round for Miss Parks, who failed to show up. After supper I made two trips to the canteen with Watling, who is sending boxes to the boys. I mailed my locket to Ray tonight. No dancing tonight as there is a bridge table on.

TUESDAY, NOVEMBER 9

A rainy morning again but less cold than our previous wet days. Off from 10–3, wrote home and went to the canteen for butter for our kitchen. The flowers in our ante tent are still very lovely. Miss Austin is certainly an adept. The asters remind me of Aunt Janet's garden, and we get such fine colors here. It has turned into a very cold rain again.

WEDNESDAY, NOVEMBER 10

Watling and Lill and I took our half days and went to Paris Plage on the bus. I am on duty in the supply tent now. Did not accomplish much in PP. Got a pair of warm gloves. It was very windy and cold, and we had another rainy night. We had a long wait for the bus at Étaples where the usual multitude of children entertained us.

THURSDAY, NOVEMBER 11

Dancing class tonight. Col. Yates admitted to F—indigestion. Another rainy day. Came off at 3 p.m. to assist Miss Austin in sandwich making. Cooper also joined in. It is officially slated that our unit is to move. But where to nobody knows. This hospital has been condemned for a winter camp. We are all very anxious that our unit should not be divided. No. 23 (or 28 BGH) is still the popular rumor. Boulogne also thought.

FRIDAY, NOVEMBER 12

Still another stormy day following a wild night. The day's rain was in showers, fast and furious. I help dismantle Ward P and make supplies. Engelke[82] and Miss Lindsay and Fitzie[83] are sent to No. 1 till Monday. They had a convoy of 400, and their staff of nurses are rather small. Where are we to go? Montreuil, Étaples, Boulogne, Hardelot, Rouen, or England. If only they will not split us up or take our boys from us.

SATURDAY, NOVEMBER 13

A day full of rumors, which elated and depressed us in turn. Miss Brand and I are to dismantle E tomorrow. A cold day and rainy at intervals. After tea, Clare and I tramped to St. Gabriel Plage. The tide was going out, but there was a fine swell on. Ward C is closed. A has one patient. G, K, L, and F are the only remaining wards with patients.

SUNDAY, NOVEMBER 14

No definite rumor today. Boulogne, Montreuil equally. *McGilliken* bright and clever today. A lovely bright fall today. Went to 10:30 service in F and spent the rest of the a.m. packing E. Went wheeling after 3 p.m. with Miss Brand and Miss

Steel to Neufchâtel. Miss Parks and Miss Carr-Harris came to tea and remained for dinner. Matron, Lill, Watling, and Clare and I walked part way home with them. The English Tommies were very noisy and rude on the road, a result, we think, from the rum found on the shore from the A.S.C.[84]

MONDAY, NOVEMBER 15

A good windy day. The supply room busy and noisy as usual and the staff greatly increased as most of the wards are closed. Walked into Camiers after tea to find some apples and went to a concert given by the 25th in the evening. Hallie Carmau began a dancing lesson afterwards, but officers came in and spoiled it all. Got a letter from home tonight.

TUESDAY, NOVEMBER 16

Prince Vic concert in the YMCA—very good. A cold morning and the ground covered with snow and still falling. In the supply room as usual. Off duty after second dinner and Lill, Watling, and Clare and I went to Paris Plage on the No. 2 bus. Got the wherewithal to clothe myself as a Poppy for the boys' party on Thursday. We had an omelet etc. at the "Toos" in Étaples while waiting for the bus. It is a wonderful place with its paintings and associations and its lovely kitchen. I have missed a great deal not having been there before.

WEDNESDAY, NOVEMBER 17

Clare and I went to Paris Plage in the a.m. to return the wheels. A cold morning but fine. Came to Étaples on the 11:30 car to find no bus running, so we walked home with the exception of a lift in an ambulance. No rain all day but it is cold and raw. Latest rumour says the Indian hospital[85] at Boulogne. All hospitals in camp except 18 and 20 have orders to pack.

THURSDAY, NOVEMBER 18

No. 18 has packing orders too. The boys' party came off with fine style. It was well arranged, the supper tent particularly so, and the costumes were wonderful considering the materials at hand. Brand dressed me as a poppy. Watling was a water lily and Lill was a cornflower. No new rumours today. Boulogne very popular yet. Col. Yates the only remaining patient. A rainy afternoon.

FRIDAY, NOVEMBER 19

28 of No. 25 busses went to Wimereux this a.m. A very cold morning but bright and clear. Quite a heavy frost. Lill and I slept in. Twelve nurses were sent to No. 1 this afternoon. Lill, Clare, and I walked to Étaples and called on No. 1 to see Arnott. Saw Violet E. and had a chat with Miss Archibald and Patterson. Such a lovely walk home. The moon is glorious tonight. Wrote Miss Greig.

SATURDAY, NOVEMBER 20

Dickie, Stevie, Clare, and I walked to Boulogne this a.m. and had lunch at the "Pre Catelan." Got an ambulance ride back part of the way. A cold day.

SUNDAY, NOVEMBER 21

Mann,[86] Watling, Clare, Dickie, and I walked to Frencq after lunch and back to camp by the Boulogne road and Widehem. A cold grey day. Went to 5:45 service. Our winter quarters is an old monastery in Boulogne. Now used as an Indian hospital.

MONDAY, NOVEMBER 22

Col. Yates left for England today. Dickie and I went to Paris Plage and wasted the afternoon with Stephens and Tate. Had lunch at a new cafe on Rue St. Jean.

TUESDAY, NOVEMBER 23

Our ante tent is moved down to the O.R. where we are much more comfortable as there is a coal stove. Dickie and I walked down to the lake and through the dunes to the sea and along back by St. Gabriel Plage.

WEDNESDAY, NOVEMBER 24

A nice day. Clare, Dickie, MacConnell, and Watling and I walked to Neufchâtel and had tea at "Prendecours." A lovely walk. Clare and I walked round the lake in the early afternoon.

THURSDAY, NOVEMBER 25

A cold day but bright. McConnell and Dickie and Watling and I went to Montreuil in the "Ford." We walked on the ramparts, did a little shopping, and had tea at the Hotel la France. Got home just as it started to rain.

FRIDAY, NOVEMBER 26

Very cold with snow flurries. We sat around in the O.R. most of the day. Clare went to Paris Plage for her glasses, and Dickie and I went to Étaples. Walked back with Miss Carpenter in an hour and ten minutes. A beautiful night but very cold. Lily Carter came to see us today.

SATURDAY, NOVEMBER 27

"Did up" a box of eats for Murray and mailed the *McGillikens* to Ray and a magazine to Greig. A letter from Ray this evening. The fourth-year boys are going home after all. We gave them and their friends a little farewell dance tonight in the O.R., a very enjoyable affair. Stevie and I went to Étaples for the cake.

SUNDAY, NOVEMBER 28

An extremely cold day. Nothing thawed. Service in the a.m. as usual, and Clare and I went on the hills after till lunch time. Wrote home and sent Ray's letter on to Len. Went to 5:45 service and Clare and I spent the evening reading "The Double Traitor."[87] A terrible night for our men in the trenches. Sisters Pidegon, MacDermid, Bliss, and Eastwood went on leave.

MONDAY, NOVEMBER 29

Rained steadily all day but not so cold. Reported that the sisters are to be billeted in Boulogne till our hospital is ready for us. Spent most of the day in the O.R. I ripped the red from my shoulder straps. (great work)

TUESDAY, NOVEMBER 30

A warmer a.m. but showery. McConnell and Gourlay[88] and I walked round the village before lunch as the O.R. is closed to us. Fixed Clare's shoulder straps this afternoon.

As December begins, Ruth is in a sad and melancholy mood. Captain Russell is being transferred, the fourth-year medical students who have been serving as orderlies are being sent back to Canada to complete their training, and the fate of the nurses is up in the air. Ruth concludes "Truly the bottom is falling out of our unit." This mood is well reflected in a poem that appears in both Ruth's and Clare's diaries.

Oh to be a turtle, a slow lethargic turtle
With nothing in the world to do
But roam around the whole day through
To sun oneself upon a log

To idly gossip with a frog
To wallow in a marshy pool
Among the reeds and rushes cool.
To feel no matter what befell
One need but crawl within one's shell
And let the whole world go to ______.

Change is imminent, for on the sixth, orders are received for both Ruth and Clare to be among fifteen nurses sent to the Canadian Red Cross's Duke of Connaught Hospital. Located on a posh estate in Taplow, England, known as Cliveden, this is to be a temporary posting. While the workload at Cliveden is lighter than in France, their reception is cool. It is described by another McGill Unit nurse as having "a Queen Anne front and a Mary Ann back," meaning the place looked much better than it really was. Having come from coveted postings in France, Ruth feels that they are resented by both the nurses and doctors at Cliveden. Unfortunately, their residence is literally as cool as their welcome, for although there are fireplaces, the nurses are not permitted to light them until after 5:00 p.m. There are, however, advantages. The resort town of Maidenhead is only a taxi ride or a short walk away, and London is not far by train. Indeed, Ruth spends her Christmas on leave in London. From there she even manages a trip south to the great training camp at Bramshott and visits her brother Len who has just arrived in England on November 9 as part of the 55th Infantry Battalion.

WEDNESDAY, DECEMBER 1

No entry

THURSDAY, DECEMBER 2

And now our fourth-year men have been given the opportunity of going home to finish. Truly the bottom is falling out of our unit. Capt. Russell is transferred to the R.A.M.C. and is to be at [space left blank]. He left us today. I got tea this afternoon. Letter from Ray tonight.

FRIDAY, DECEMBER 3

Rained all day. Dickie and I spent the a.m. doing up cards. And I wrote Mrs. Young and Len. Posted parcels to Ray and one to Greig. Mrs. Brand and Clare and I read "The Four Maries"[89] and had such a nice time.

SATURDAY, DECEMBER 4

Another rainy day. Settled with Suzanne, a big business. The billet rumor is current again. Clare and I walked to No. 1 and had tea in the club with Miss Cooper. Huts here are nearly finished and we are wondering if we will move in.

SUNDAY, DECEMBER 5

Went to morning service and wrote home in the afternoon. Our mess tent blew down and we have moved into the new hut though the carpenters are still at work there. Our batmen "struck" work this a.m. and got marched back by Sgt. M. Kennedy.

MONDAY, DECEMBER 6

Like a bolt from the blue we got orders to proceed to Cliveden. Clare and I among fifteen, and fifteen others to go to Shorncliffe. We are to go on Wednesday. Clare and I went to Paris Plage on errands and, of course, it rained. Sent an extra card in my letter home telling them of our move.

TUESDAY, DECEMBER 7

A rainy day. Everyone is depressed and we are very sad at leaving. The fifth-year men left us today. That is the first big break-up, and our going will be the next. Watling remains in France.

WEDNESDAY, DECEMBER 8

A beautiful a.m. for our leaving. We left our lovely hills with regret. It will be like going home if we return. The boys gave us a fine McGill yell and off we went. The fifth-year men crossed from Boulogne with us. A terrible crossing. Nearly everyone seasick, including Dickie and Clare. Came to London and will remain here all tomorrow.

THURSDAY, DECEMBER 9

Miss Steel and Lindsay remain in London to look after our luggage. Got up for breakfast and Lill and I took a trip to the bank and who should come across but Bun Creaghan.[90] Len has just left London from a six-day leave. We came down here on the 11 o'clock train and as yet feel like strangers in a strange land. Rooming with seven other girls.

FRIDAY, DECEMBER 10

Went on duty in our new uniforms with borrowed aprons and bibs and veils as our baggage has not come yet. Would that Miss MacLatchy could see us. I am in H2, Lill just across in H1. Dick and I have 1–4 off and we went to see Cliveden House, about a half mile from here. It is all very lovely, but I have no eye for England yet.

SATURDAY, DECEMBER 11

Clare and Dick and I took a taxi into Maidenhead and got some Xmas cards. It is a relief to get away from the atmosphere

here. We seem to be rather resented and the MDs are none too friendly. Miss Drake goes on night duty tonight. She with her usual wit describes this place as having a "Queen Anne front and a Mary Ann back."

SUNDAY, DECEMBER 12

A very cold a.m. with snow. The wards are bitterly cold and this lodge is without heat except for grate fires, and we are not allowed to light them until 5 p.m. It is rather a cheerless place on the whole. Letter from home today, redirected from No. 3. Clare and I went walking in our off hours to Burnham[91] and around home by a different route.

MONDAY, DECEMBER 13

A convoy came to us today of something over a hundred. No bad cases came to H2. Patients from Rouen and Boulogne.

TUESDAY, DECEMBER 14

Had half days and Dickie, Clare, Brad, and I went to London. I had a sick headache so did not enjoy the p.m. much. We did some shopping (in the rain). Had dinner at Frescalis and went to see "Mavourneen," which was fairly good. Came home on the midnight train. Letter from Len and Miss Richardson and a box of Page and Shaw[92] from Laura.

WEDNESDAY, DECEMBER 15

Wrote Len and Gourlay. Had hours 1–4. Lill and I went to the Glory Hole and got our blankets etc. from our kits. It is quite as damp a storeroom as the old bell tent. Found Miss Wood's cousin, such a nice boy. Also found a Chatham boy, Ullock,[93] who looks sixteen and has a tb hip. Poor lad. A rainy day.

THURSDAY, DECEMBER 16

Lill and I got a lovely box of Scotch cakes from Mrs. Greig and handkerchiefs from Miss Blackwood. Miss Watson has her p.m. and I had hours 2–5. Miss Nichol is with us today. Miss Ramsay and she exchanged.

FRIDAY, DECEMBER 17

Lill and I walked to Maidenhead in last hours.[94] Got cards and I ordered a cake to be sent to Murray. Also got sundries and smokes for them. 7 lbs[95] is the limit to go and it soon mounts up. We had a lovely walk both ways as there wasn't a taxi to be had. Quite a relief to get away from here for a time. Another convoy today.

SATURDAY, DECEMBER 18

Walked to town again with Clare but taxied home to go on duty at 4. Mailed our parcels. Things as usual in the ward.

SUNDAY, DECEMBER 19

Intended to go out with Clare, but our hours did not agree. Wrote home.

MONDAY, DECEMBER 20

Ward decorations have begun. Jenkins (Canadian) is directing things from bed 46. English Ivy and paper flowers are much in evidence.

TUESDAY, DECEMBER 21

Miss Nichols had her p.m. and we were quite busy.

WEDNESDAY, DECEMBER 22

Miss Watson's day off. She is feeling very miserable. I had first hours. Our ward is looking pretty. More like April than Xmas.

THURSDAY, DECEMBER 23

On duty as usual and the Xmas decorations still going up. Jenkins is very miserable and not up to his usual.

FRIDAY, DECEMBER 24

On duty in the a.m. and got the 1 p.m. train to London. Put up at the Kingsley. Jane Todd here too. We went shopping in the rain and went to see "Stop Thief" at the Prince of Wales Theatre. Screamingly funny. We will have a good sleep in the a.m.

SATURDAY, DECEMBER 25

Rather a wonderful day. We went to St. Paul's for the 10:30 service and saw Dr. Enright[96] who took us to lunch in Charing Cross and then for sightseeing. Everything closed so we contented ourselves with seeing London from the top of buses. Finished up the day with dinner at the Frascati, all at Dr. E.'s expense. Met Jack and Gordon Hunter and Desbrasy[97] and Boysie Wood. Clare gave me "Tale of Two Cities" for a Xmas gift, and we each had wee booklets from Edith Stewart. Clare went to early services and we had breakfast in bed.

SUNDAY, DECEMBER 26

Dickie and I went to Bramshott by the 8:40 train. Len met us and we walked the three miles to camp. Had dinner in the sergeants' mess and walked back to Hazelmore for the 4:44 train back to London. Not a drop of rain all day.

MONDAY, DECEMBER 27

Lill and I went to see Grace and Wallie and then called at the Abbey for Clare. Home to the Kingsley where Dr. Enright joined us for lunch. Went to the zoo and then for a bus ride across the Thames and back by Tower Bridge. Dinner at Franscati's and to the New Theatre to see *Peter Pan*.

TUESDAY, DECEMBER 28

Found a letter from Alice K. and a field card from Murray. It's very hard going back to work. Had last hours. Miss Ramsay has gone to Shorncliffe quite suddenly.

WEDNESDAY, DECEMBER 29

Started work in H2 but sent to Annex with Miss Kirk. 722 patients, a good many of them convalescent. A lot more men, but Miss Kirk is very poor. Was left alone all p.m. and found it very hard to find out what work was to be done. No hours off. Letters from Aunt Blanche, Ray, Mrs. Loggie, Mrs. Young and cards from several other people.

THURSDAY, DECEMBER 30

Am back in H2 as Miss Nichols is off with a boil. It is good to be back with nice Miss Watson. Did the usual dressings all a.m. and had first hours. Wrote Alice K. with many interruptions.

FRIDAY, DECEMBER 31

Miss Watson went on leave and I am in charge in the meantime. Miss Nichols may be in tomorrow. Had morning hours and wrote Miss Hepburn. No letters.

NOTES

1 Christina Watling of Chatham, NB, Lillian Dickie of River Charlo, NB, and Clare Gass of Shubenacadie, NS.

2 Mufti refers to civilian clothing as opposed to their military uniforms.

3 Jennette Duncan, born Montreal 1877, graduated from Montreal General Hospital (MGH) 1904, and enlisted in the CAMC April 22, 1915.

4 Isabel Davies, born Montreal 1881, graduated MGH 1908, and enlisted in CAMC April 22, 1915.

5 The 21st Infantry Battalion, raised in Eastern Ontario, sailed aboard the Metagama. Clare Gass also mentions that both the Fourth (French Canadian) and Fifth (Queen's) Stationary Hospitals were on board.

6 Graduates of the MGH against those of the Royal Victoria Hospital (RVH), the two source hospitals for the McGill Unit's nurses.

7 Dickie is Ruth's persistent nickname for her friend Lillian Dickie.

8 Apparently both Beatrice Armitage of Sherbroke and Eleanor Handcock of Montreal were very seasick.

9 Katerine Osborne MacLatchy, born 1874 in Grand Pré, NS, enlisted May 4, 1915, as Matron of No. 3 CGH.

10 Alexander Watling (46798) joined the Canadian Expeditionary Force (CEF) in Sept. 1914, was wounded (gunshot, left hand) in Feb. 1915, and was recuperating at the American Women's Red Cross Hospital at Paignton, England.

11 McEwen, In The Company of Nurses, 113.

12 Clare Gass diary (CGD), May 27, 1915.

13 Evertta Watters, born Montreal 1883, graduated MGH 1910, and enlisted in CAMC April 22, 1915.

14 Louise McGreer, born Napanee, ON, 1877, graduated MGH 1912, and enlisted in CAMC April 22, 1915.

15 Ethel Frances Upton, born 1883 at Montreal, enlisted in CAMC Feb. 1915 at Halifax.

16 Cecily Galt, born Toronto 1888, enlisted in CAMC at Touquet, France, Jan. 22, 1915.

17 Juliet Marie Pelletier, born Quebec 1890, enlisted CAMC Sept. 26, 1914.

18 Nursing Sisters Cora Peters Archibald (born Truro, NS, 1881, graduated RVH 1909, enlisted May 5, 1915) and Maud Emilie Austin (born London, England, graduated RVH 1912, enlisted in CAMC April 22, 1915), both temporarily reposted from the McGill Unit to Rouen.

19 William C. Archibald (314) of Wolfville, NS, had been a medical student at McGill and was now serving as an orderly.

20 Margaret Woods, born Welsford, NB, 1883, graduated RVH 1914, and enlisted in CAMC April 15, 1915.

21 Victoria Eastwood, born Mamora, ON, 1885, graduated RVH 1909, and enlisted in CAMC May 4, 1915.

22 Annette Tate, born 1887 in Jamaica, graduated MGH 1914, and joined the CAMC April 22, 1915.

23 Margaret MacIntosh, born Halifax 1885, graduated RVH 1902, enlisted CAMC April 22, 1915.

24 Most likely Ruth's first cousin Laura Anderson, born 1889.

25 Sara Chisholm, born 1888, Florence, Wisconsin, graduated RVH 1914, enlisted in CAMC April 22, 1915.

26 A misspelling of trephine, a special cylindrical saw for cutting into the skull.
27 CGD, June 8 and 9, 1915.
28 Murray MacLaren, born Richibucto, NB, 1861, a surgeon who joined in Sept. 1914.
29 Lilly Naomi Gray, born Montreal 1883, graduated MGH 1913, and joined the CAMC April 22, 1915.
30 Major Edouard Lebel, born 1865, Quebec, a physician, joined CEF Sept. 1914.
31 Goodwin's was a large Montreal department store (also mail order) bought out by Eaton's in the postwar era.
32 Col. Herbert S. Birkett, Officer Commanding, No. 3 Canadian General Hospital, the McGill Unit.
33 Jessie M. Sedgewick, born Middle Musquodobit, NS, 1890, graduated RVH 1914, joined CAMC April 22, 1915.
34 Written by W. D. Craufurd, E. Monton, and E. A. Manton, Peeps into Picardy (London: Simpkin, Marshall, Hamilton, Kent & Co., Ltd, 1914) is a tourist guide not only listing sites of interest, but also including tales of history, religion, and warfare.
35 Edna Jane Giffin, a widow, born Port Hood, NS, 1881, graduated MGH 1913, enlisted CAMC April 22, 1915.
36 Mary F. Steele, born Brockville, ON, 1876, graduated RVH 1892, enlisted in CAMC May 4, 1915.
37 Frank Ullock (23587) of Chatham, NB, wounded in right knee at Givenchy June 15, arrived at No 1 CGH two days later and had his leg amputated above the knee. Ruth mentions him for he was from her part of New Brunswick.
38 CGD, July 10, 1915.
39 CGD, July 29, 1915.
40 Jean Bell, born Carleton Place, ON, 1878, enlisted CAMC Sept. 25, 1914, at Quebec.
41 Mary Bliss, born Ottawa 1882, graduated RVH 1911, enlisted April 22, 1915.
42 Possibly Jean Loggie, aged twenty-two of Chatham and Maggie Loggie, thirty-three, wife of William of Burnt Church.
43 Ray (also, sometimes, Rae) is Rachael, Ruth's older sister, born 1880, and Len is Leonard, her younger brother, born 1889.
44 Most likely Ruth's younger sister Helen, born 1891.
45 Lilian Pidgeon, born Kensington, PEI, 1888, graduated RVH 1913, enlisted April 15, 1915, and Hope Sewell, born Belleville, ON, 1891, graduated RVH 1914, enlisted April 22, 1915.
46 Mabel Lindsay, born Ottawa 1874, graduated RVH 1898, enlisted in CAMC April 22, 1915.
47 Alice Stewart, born Glasgow, Scotland, 1886, graduated RVH 1913, enlisted in CAMC April 16, 1915.
48 Louise M. Stevens, born Wallace Grant, NS, 1888, graduated MGH 1914, enlisted April 22, 1915, and Ellen E Carpenter, born Rome, Italy, 1889, graduated RVH 1914, enlisted April 22, 1915.
49 This "Tina" appears to be Ruth's new nickname for Christina Watling.
50 A heavy cotton fabric, often with a floral pattern, used for upholstery.
51 Harriet Carman, born Winnipeg 1885, graduated MGH 1910, enlisted in CAMC April 22, 1915.

52 Occasionally and very sparingly, much coveted green envelopes, similar to airmail envelopes, were issued. Although limited in actual size, they were exempt from the prying eyes of the censors.
53 Most likely the wounded soldier from Montreal mentioned on June 12 as "Dalhman."
54 More likely F. I. Gertrude De Cow, born Montreal 1888, graduated MGH 1913, enlisted April 22, 1915.
55 Eveline M. Whitney, born Wimbledon, England, 1889, graduated MGH 1913, enlisted in CAMC April 2, 1915.
56 Bertha Forgey, born Saint John, NB, 1882, graduated RVH 1909, enlisted April 16, 1915.
57 Constance Harrison, born Leeds, England, 1888, graduated RVH 1910, enlisted April 22, 1915.
58 Nellie Elizabeth Louise MacDonald, born Chatham, NB, 1883, enlisted in CAMC May 12, 1915.
59 CGD, August 26, 1915.
60 Assistant Director Medical Services.
61 Sam Hughes (1853–1921), Canadian Minister of Militia and Defense in the Conservative government of Sir Robert Borden. A great advocate of the pre-war militia, wartime military, and all things Imperial but as a fervent Canadian nationalist who believed the British could learn a thing or two from colonials, and Canadians in particular.
62 Louise F. McLeod, born Woodstock, ON, 1882, graduated MGH 1908, enlisted in CAMC April 22, 1915.
63 Moise W. Le Bel (385), born Ottawa 1892, a member of the McGill Unit who listed his occupation as "medical student."
64 The World was the local Chatham, NB, newspaper published every Wednesday and Saturday.
65 The McGill Unit also took in members of the local French population who were ill.
66 Victor Lapp (382) was a McGill student who joined the unit on April 15, 1915. He worked as an orderly.
67 Clare records that Col. McCrae's lecture was on the Second Battle of Ypres (CGD, Sept. 17, 1915).
68 Rachael McConnell, born Ireland 1886, graduated MGH 1914, enlisted in CAMC April 22, 1915; Alice M. Stewart, born Glasgow, Scotland, 1886, graduated RVH 1913, enlisted in CAMC April 16, 1915; Dorothy Cotton, born Quebec 1886, graduated RVH 1910, enlisted in CAMC May 4, 1915.
69 Ruth's cousin Helen M. Loggie was married to Robert Donald, bank manager, on Sept. 6, 1915, and Ruth's sister Ray served as bridesmaid.
70 Due to the horridly harsh and unsanitary conditions of Lemnos in the Mediterranean, Matron Jessie Jaggard and Nursing Sister Mary F. Munro both died of dysentery at No. 1 CGH in Sept. 1915.
71 Louise J. Brand, born Ellershouse, NS, 1881, graduated RVH 1909, enlisted CAMC April 22, 1915.
72 Potash and Perlmutter was an American three-act comedy about the clothing industry written by Montague Glass and Charles Klien. Originally produced on Broadway, a production opened in London on April 14, 1914.
73 Channell G. Hepburn, Anglican chaplain, born Magog, PQ, 1888, enlisted Aug. 1915.

74 Nursing Sister Margaret Hamilton, part of the volunteer American "Chicago Hospital" serving with the British Army in France. She contracted meningitis and died within thirty-six hours.
75 Jane Glendenning, born Manilla, ON,1885, graduated RVH 1914, enlisted in CAMC April 16, 1915.
76 Howard C. Dixon, born Maple Creek, SK, 1886, physician, enlisted CAMC April 7, 1915.
77 Louella Louise Gillis, born Tide Head, NB, 1884, graduated MGH 1909, enlisted in CAMC April 22, 1915.
78 Alice M. Cooper, born in England, graduated MGH 1912, enlisted CAMC April 22, 1915.
79 Harriet Drake, born in Utah, graduated RVH 1907, enlisted in CAMC April 22, 1915.
80 Wib is actually Wilbur, Ruth's older brother.
81 Eva Bradley, born Eardley, PQ, 1886, graduated RVH 1910, enlisted CAMC April 14, 1915.
82 Mary E. Engelke, born Montreal 1883, graduated MGH 1912, enlisted in CAMC April 13, 1915.
83 Olive Fitzgibbon, born Montreal 1884, graduated RVH 1913, enlisted in CAMC April 14, 1915.
84 Army Service Corps.
85 A hospital dedicated to the troops from India serving on the Western Front.
86 Jane F. Mann, born Shigawake, PQ, 1889, graduated MGH 1914, enlisted in CAMC April 22, 1915.
87 A very popular Great War spy novel by Edward Phillips Oppenheim.
88 Roberta Gourlay, born Eaganville, ON, graduated MGH 1914, enlisted CAMC April 22, 1915.
89 A popular literary work about the four ladies-in-waiting to Mary, Queen of Scots.
90 Most likely Thomas Creaghan of Newcastle, NB, who was an officer in the 55th Battalion, the same unit as Ruth's brother Len.
91 At least a nine-kilometre walk.
92 A box of chocolates from this famous New England candy company.
93 See note 91.
94 A round trip of at least eight miles or thirteen kilometres.
95 Maximum parcel weight allowed by the postal service.
96 William James Enright of Quebec who was recovering from injuries at Shorncliffe Camp in England.
97 Perhaps Merrill DesBrisay (411038), who listed his occupation as McGill student on his attestation papers.

The War Diary of Ruth Loggie

1916

A new year of war begins and Ruth is still at Taplow, England. While the nursing duties are not that taxing, Ruth finds the atmosphere of the place oppressive. Two of the resident nurses have a blow-up on the second and refuse to speak to each other the next day. Not surprisingly, the O.C. (Officer Commanding) visits the following day and states that "the beds looked as if the wrath of God had struck them." His message: stick to your work duties and stop fighting among yourselves. It does not help Ruth that rumours continue to swirl concerning the relocation of the McGill Unit in France. With the passage of time however, a location in Boulogne is looking ever more likely.

As a break from Cliveden, Ruth takes up birdwatching and golf, or as she calls it, "trench digging," and she continues to explore. She and a few others go on an outing to Windsor Castle. It should be noted that when her spirits are low, her diary entries become shorter. Correspondingly, her letter writing to those at home increases as she has extra time. It is also evident throughout her diary that the importance of receiving letters and parcels from home never abates. Her animated comments on the nurses receiving their "McGill Christmas box," though a month late, are a case in point. They gain entry into the well boxed case with shovel, fireplace tongs, and a poker.

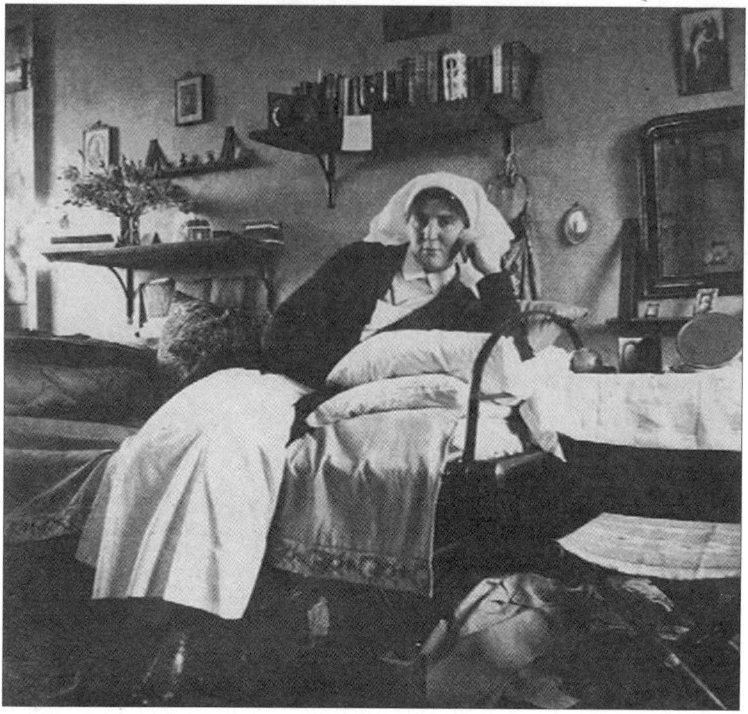

A tired Ruth relaxing in her room in France.

SATURDAY, JANUARY 1

Miss Nichols on deck again. Everything goes smoothly and I serve dinners at noon. Had early p.m. and wrote Effie Brown. News from Camiers says that instead of moving to Boulogne we are to take over No. 22 and get to work as soon as possible

SUNDAY, JANUARY 2

Off for last hours and wrote home. Nothing happens and no news from Len. A card from Naomi Gray. No fresh news. The climax is reached this a.m. between Mrs. Burns and Mrs. MacLachlan and the air was blue and frosty. Mrs. Burns came off second best.

MONDAY, JANUARY 3

The O.C. and the matron visited our ward this morning, and the O.C. said that beds looked as though the wrath of God had struck them. Lill is on night duty tonight and I feel very lonely. No mail today. Silence between Mrs. Burns and Mrs. MacLachlan tonight.

TUESDAY, JANUARY 4

No news of any description, and this room is very tiresome. Have tried all evening to write a letter and found it impossible.

WEDNESDAY, JANUARY 5

Got a box of fudge tonight from Helen Loggie. Had my p.m. today and spent it in bed I was so tired. No letters from home this week.

THURSDAY, JANUARY 6

Miss Nichols and I started a round of golf with Sergeant Falconer. We did the first hole and then deserted the course and went bird hunting. The sergeant is an authority on the subject and most entertaining, and we had a lovely walk. Had a letter from Len saying he will not come down.

FRIDAY, JANUARY 7

On duty tonight. Had the p.m. off. Miss Davies, McLeod, and Armitage[1] were down to see. They tell us (also had a card from Watling to this effect) that our headquarters have been moved to Boulogne and we are not to occupy No. 22 after all. We moved to the old cottage. Clare and I room just across from Dickie. One more move added to our many moves.

SATURDAY, JANUARY 8

Wrote to Mrs. Park, Mrs. Dearin, and Grace Loggie and Helen Donald. The ward is very light just now.

SUNDAY, JANUARY 9

A convoy came in this evening. I got ten—trench foot and debilets.[2] Not a dressing among them. Webb is to be operated on tomorrow. Wrote Ray. No home letters yet.

MONDAY, JANUARY 10

Got such a nice letter from Mrs. Sutherland and cards from Miss Harrington and K. Brook. No letter from home yet. Webb's condition is very poor. White is in the clink tonight. Refused to come back to the ward to finish his work. I have Frenchie for the night. Lill is reporting Gordon in the a.m.

TUESDAY, JANUARY 11

White is back on duty. Cheerful and apparently well pleased with himself. Webb is better tonight. Wrote Harold. Clare and a couple of patients and I played golf or rather dug trenches. A beautiful a.m. Went to see a little chapel on the estate.

WEDNESDAY, JANUARY 12

Nice letters from home, one from May, a card from Aunt J. and Uncle W., and a note from Grace[3] saying we will be down on Friday. Also a letter from Len. I sent an additional book to him this a.m.

THURSDAY, JANUARY 13

Such a cold night. White frost on the ground. Hargreaves groaned all night with his hand. I got a second box from home—fudge and chocolate from Aunt Kate. Got two letters from Len written in August. Another from Mrs. Youngsley. They have been travelling.

FRIDAY, JANUARY 14

Grace came down at 2:30. Clare and Lill and Miss Nichols and Miss Whitlock and I met her, and we motored to Stoke Poges and then on to Windsor.[4] A perfect afternoon. Saw Wm. Penn's church and I would call it Grey's church tower and church yard. Such a dear, quiet, restful spot. Dickie and Miss W. shopped in Windsor, and we went to the castle.

SATURDAY, JANUARY 15

Had nice tea and cakes for 9 d.[5]

SUNDAY, JANUARY 16

Wrote Ray as usual.

MONDAY, JANUARY 17

Six of us motored into Maidenhead and back. I got my snaps and ordered more. White did the socks and laundry.

TUESDAY, JANUARY 18

Mr. Corry Clark[6] came down to see me today. He is sailing for Home this week and will phone Papa. Two boxes of chocolates came from Aunt B. and Uncle J.

WEDNESDAY, JANUARY 19

Four of the girls went riding this morning, and we waited up to see them off. Both Alice Stuart and Edith Leslie[7] got thrown but were not hurt.

THURSDAY, JANUARY 20

Wrote Len, Bernice, Mrs. Sadler, and a card to Aunt B., Dickie, Miss Moore, and Miss V., and I walked to Maidenhead and taxied back. Got a letter direct from Ray today.[8]

FRIDAY, JANUARY 21

Edith Stewart is quite ill, and Bran is specializing her tonight. Letter from Laura today and wrote her tonight.

SATURDAY, JANUARY 22

No entry

SUNDAY, JANUARY 23

No entry

MONDAY, JANUARY 24

Clare, Lill, and I walked to Maidenhead by the river. A lovely walk and taxied back. Lill and I were measured for uniforms, and Clare left her dress to be fixed.

TUESDAY, JANUARY 25

No orderly tonight and no socks done.

WEDNESDAY, JANUARY 26

A letter from Len this a.m. saying he has the measles.

THURSDAY, JANUARY 27

No entry

FRIDAY, JANUARY 28

No entry

SATURDAY, JANUARY 29

Our McGill box of Xmas things came this a.m. Great fun opening it as the batmen were too busy reading their mail to attend to it. The poker and tongs and an old shovel were brought into use and we managed beautifully.[9]

JANUARY 29–FEBRUARY 3

No entries

Ruth begins February in a drab mood, dreading a return to France while at the same time living on rumours as to when the return will happen. The only bright spot is their proximity to London and the chance to enjoy live theatre like Puss and Boots. Finally, on the fifteenth, rumour turns to orders–they are returning to France. By the twentieth, Ruth and Clare are walking to see Napoleon's Monument from their new home at No. 3 CGH on the outskirts of Boulogne. The McGill Unit has relocated to the grounds of the ruins of an abandoned former Jesuit college and monastery. Both their living quarters and the patient wards are flimsy wooden huts. The days are cold and miserable, and everybody is shivering. It then snows several times. The storm on the twenty-fifth is significant enough to be compared to those of Canada, with both Ruth and Clare commenting that it is deep enough for sleighs. Despite a double ration of oil for their stoves, Ruth confides to her diary on the twenty-sixth that she "suffer(s) agonies of the damned tonight." The weather has become their newest and fiercest enemy.

FRIDAY, FEBRUARY 4

Wrote Naomi Gray tonight. We feel very low in our minds about returning to France. No news and no letters. Clare and I took a few snapshots before going to bed.[10]

SATURDAY, FEBRUARY 5

Went for uniform fittings this a.m. Miss Moore walked with us by the river road. Such a beautiful morning, and the woods look like spring. So many green shoots. I brought my Dickens home and am so glad to have them. We taxied home after noon. Have a letter from Victor Lapp tonight. No fresh news. The Arnoldi sisters, Kitty and Helen,[11] arrived today and are attached here.

SUNDAY, FEBRUARY 6

Wrote Ray as usual. No letter yet. Nell Tuck came from London to see us. She has joined the QA Reserve[12] nursing sisters and looks well and happy. Clare went to see Station with her, and her bus broke down on the way and she came home by pony cart.

MONDAY, FEBRUARY 7

Off night duty. Clare and Lill and I went up to London on the 10:15 train, returning by the 5:05. We shopped and lunched at the Army and Navy Stores and went to see "Puss in Boots" at Drury Lane theatre. Such a very pretty play and a long performance. The butterfly drill and dance is wonderful, and the costumes so lovely. We got home in time for first dinner. No letters yet. A letter from Len this a.m. saying he was leaving Bramshott for Shorncliffe. Mrs. B. trial today.[13]

TUESDAY, FEBRUARY 8

I indulged in a sick headache and spent my hours off in bed. I am in H3 with Miss Nichols. Miss Watson took my place on night duty. Still no letters. Mrs. B's trial still on. A letter from Aunt Mamie tonight from N.C.

WEDNESDAY, FEBRUARY 9

Spent my hours off—5 off. Moving my trunk from the cottage to our room. After many trips with the contents, Lill assisted with the trunk.

THURSDAY, FEBRUARY 10

Miss Nichols' half day off, and she just learned that she and Miss Hamilton are to leave on Saturday. They go to a Convalescent Hospital at Wolkingham. I will miss her very much. Had morning hours. The B affair still goes on and will go on. It is a terrible tragedy. The trial is just put off, to continue on Monday. Mrs. Astor presented Queen A.'s gift books, "The Way of the Red Cross," to us today after lunch.

FRIDAY, FEBRUARY 11

My half day and Clare's. Dickie, being a charge sister, had to remain on for a convoy, which is to come in this afternoon. We had a pony cart drive to Burnham beaches planned, but the rainy afternoon put that off. Have been writing letters by Clare's fire. One from Ray today. An old one redirected from No. 3. Wrote Lapp and Len and a card to Ben Goulay and did up a book for Wib and magazine for Papa and a picture of "Hard Times" and Barnaby Ridge for Ray. Clare and I walked by the Boston Estate before tea.

SATURDAY, FEBRUARY 12

Alone in H2 till 2 p.m. so had a busy time. One of the recent Laval sisters with me. A letter from Alice K. today.

SUNDAY, FEBRUARY 13 / MONDAY, FEBRUARY 14

Off from 4 p.m. and Dickie and I took tea with Edith Stuart. The occasion being her birthday. Wrote home in the evening. Terrible tragedy in Alex this a.m.[14] This hospital is surely unlucky just now. Off duty. Edith Leslie is very miserable with her hands and is such a blowy day. Lill and I taxied into Maidenhead with our new uniforms to fix. Clare walked in and we got back in an ambulance. I ordered some cakes sent to Murray and Walter[15] and mailed my parcels. Got weighed and have gained again. A letter from Miss Tedford today. We hear that Winnie B. and B. Moores have sailed. The B affair continued today, and Miss Drake is off with a bad cold. Miss Watson is off and Crockford manages H2.

TUESDAY, FEBRUARY 15

First a rumour and then official notice that we go to France on Saturday. Edith S. goes to Isle of Wight on that day too. Most of us are very glad to get away from the investigations. A letter from Len today. He feels so disappointed in not getting out of England. They are at Westenhanger, Kent. Edith Leslie is better and will be able to cross with us. A gale and some rain today.

WEDNESDAY, FEBRUARY 16

Have a letter from Mr. Archibald tonight. No. 1 is not very busy just now, and their corps is at full strength with additions from Shorncliffe. Spent my hours off with Edith L. and Miss Drake and Miss Watson. They are better. The wind is still high, but the day was fine. New orders tonight that lights are to be darkened as much as possible. It has been wondered at that these precautions have not been taken sooner. Lill packed her trunk tonight. I wrote Miss Nichols.

THURSDAY, FEBRUARY 17

We are to go up to London after lunch tomorrow Miss Campbell says. Sister Gagne took her p.m. today and I was quite busy. Spent my morning hours writing home to Len and Grace. There was a party tonight for us, and Mrs. Phips entertained with her banjo and delightful little southern songs. She was very sweet and pretty. Had most of my packing to do tonight and am so tired.

FRIDAY, FEBRUARY 18

On duty till 11:30. Such a time saying my goodbyes. The patients hate changes in the nursing staff. We went to the station in an ambulance, and Miss Brand and Lill and I spent most of the p.m. in London getting the luggage transferred etc. Lill and I had dinner with Grace and Wallie and got to the Kingsley at bedtime. I sent a wire to Len but hardly expect to see him. Lill bought a lovely writing case. Guess I am taking a cold.

SATURDAY, FEBRUARY 19

Off at 9:15 Victoria Station. The ride to Folkstone is very pretty and it was a beautiful day. We went through the hop country, which is quite extensive. We passed right through Westenhanger, but it was too unexpected for me to keep a lookout. The wind came up directly we got on board, but the crossing was pretty smooth. One or two sick. Had lunch at the Louvre and got to camp at 4 p.m.

SUNDAY, FEBRUARY 20

Clare and I went for nice walk to Napoleon's Monument in the a.m. It is quite cold and windy. On duty in the p.m. in K2 with Miss MacIntosh and Samson and Gilles. Was quite busy. Three huts with twenty-five patients each. Miss Harkham tells me that Aunt Emma is dead.

MONDAY, FEBRUARY 21

450 patients in hospital received in five days. Such a cold place this is. We are really suffering. We are in a splendid situation for summer as far as air is concerned, but we will have every wind. The hospital is straggly, the huts are small as the ground is cut up with trees and walls in ruins. It will be lovely in summer. Our quarters are nice, but very cold and difficult to heat. I found a large box of sweets from Helen and a box of shortbread from Jessie Fowler for "the bunch," also a letter from Ray. It is a very cold night. Went into Boulogne in my hours off and bought a table and a pair of brackets.

TUESDAY, FEBRUARY 22

Such a cold miserable day. Snowing this evening. I turned our furniture round and fixed things up a bit in my hours off. 4:30 off. Suzanne is still our laundress. Am fairly busy in my ward. No mail today and I have not written home yet. Am too cold and miserable. Col. Birkett got back to us yesterday.

WEDNESDAY, FEBRUARY 23

Another cold day with rain. Lill and I had p.m. off and shopped in town. Such a funny time. We got several necessaries including a blanket to act as a rug and a pair of rubbers each. A convoy of eighty-three came in last night with some bad cases. No letters today, and another day and I haven't written even Len yet. He will be wondering what has become of me. Samson gave me quite shocking news today of M. McKechnie's death of pneumonia. Also his cousin Mrs. Wm. Davidson who lived in Westmount.

THURSDAY, FEBRUARY 24

Another very cold day following a night of misery. I will never forget these days as long as I live. No convoy last night and a large evacuation to Convalescent Camp today. Got my dress from Cliveden today and a letter from Ray. They were having soft weather at home, and the snaps and music and pictures have arrived. They are getting lots of eggs at home.

FRIDAY, FEBRUARY 25

A regular Canadian snowstorm with such drifting. Oh, for a warm Canadian house. Our ante tent is very comfortable, however. A small convoy last night of forty. I did not get any. Three local admissions today. Am as miserable as possible, and last night was a nightmare with cold and coughing. We are to be allowed a double issue of oil, so we should be warmer. Life has been difficult these days. Evacuation to hospital ship today.

SATURDAY, FEBRUARY 26

Snow enough for sleighs and less cold, and I feel better. There is a convoy tonight I hear. The hospital has 1,000 beds ready now, and there are a great number of local cases coming in. It is quite like the old MGH days. I have trench feet and suffer agonies of the damned tonight. No mail and I have never written home yet.

SUNDAY, FEBRUARY 27

Another miserable day. I was reduced to rubber boots this a.m. I replaced by black boots about noon. Had three hrs. off and Miss MacIntosh sent me off early. My uniforms arrived from Cliveden today. No laundry yet.

MONDAY, FEBRUARY 28

A beautiful a.m. but rainy later on. Have a sick headache added to my list of complaints. Took my p.m. and feel much better tonight. Sewed our muslin window curtains today. A convoy of eighty-seven last night and more local cases in. No home mail yet. Miss MacNaughton went to No. 13 General today as she is now improving. A number of the girls are off ill. The girls still in quarantine. Grouches are still in evidence.

TUESDAY, FEBRUARY 29

We hear today that Mrs. MacNaughton is to be operated on.[16] It is a perfect day, bright and warmer although very wet underfoot. Lill had her p.m. and went into town with Babbit and bought green curtain stuff and an oil can. We are beginning to be fixed up.

March begins with an influx of patients and a continuation of the horrid weather. The unit's war diary records admissions of 94, 107, 94, 45, and 107 new patients each day from the second to the seventh. Many of the sick men have trench foot from standing in slush and mud for days on end in wet boots. This leads to the rumour, which proves to be untrue, that the Germans "seeded" the trenches with saltpetre before leaving them. The men are not the only ones to suffer from the wet and muddy conditions. Ruth and Clare have to wear rubbers and black boots, and Ruth's feet are sore all month long. On top of all this, Ruth has a bad head cold and then comes down with pink eye, which is treated by being cauterized with silver nitrate. Clare confides to her diary on the twentieth that "Ruth is very miserable with a bad throat, sore eyes, and a cold and cough which she has had for a long time."[17] Not surprisingly, Ruth skips her diary entries some days.

All, however, is not misery for there is romance as well as scandal at No. 3 CGH. Nursing Sister Barbara Lamont is to resign her commission at month's end in order to be married. Much more striking, however, is the revelation that Nursing Sister Beatrice Louise Armitage and Captain Howard Dixon were secretly married before the McGill Unit left Canada! As the Canadian Army did not permit nurses to be married, Armitage has to resign. She returns to Canada and lives with her parents, where she receives her new husband's assigned pay. As for Captain Dixon, he was allowed to serve out the remainder of the war overseas. This incident typifies the period's double standard as practiced by the CAMC.

WEDNESDAY, MARCH 1

A small convoy last night. I did not get anything. Lill and I worked on our room today. We will be glad to get it tidied up. Today's news say Mrs. MacNaughton is not going to be operated on after all. Buck thinks she is foolish. No laundry yet.

THURSDAY, MARCH 2

The girls came out of quarantine last night. Frances McKeen "went in." We will have to expect frequent housings with so many local cases. The hospital is quite busy, but everything is working out quite well. My orderly is <u>no good</u> and such a trial. A fine day in spots. Whitney is off sick with cold. My feet are bad. Rubbers and black boots still necessary. I would be quite happy if not for my feet.

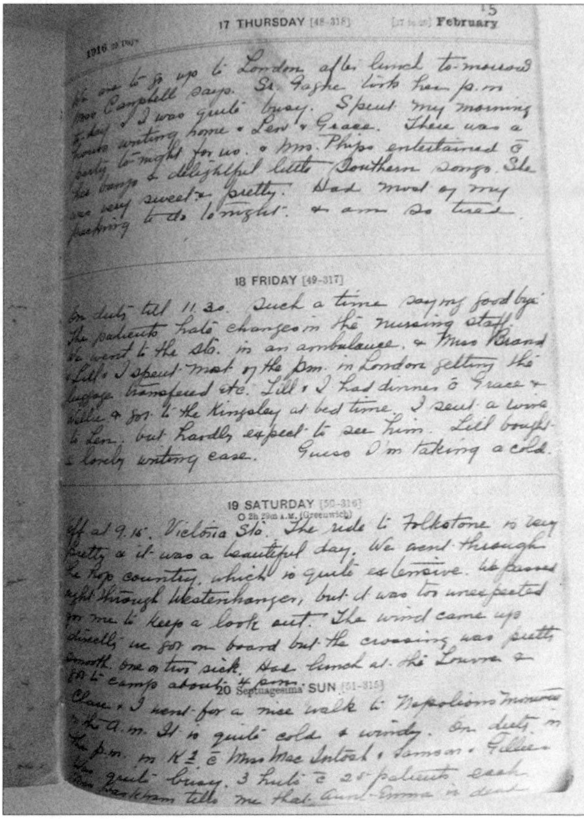

17 THURSDAY [48-318] February 1916

[illegible] are to go up to London after lunch to-morrow [illegible] Campbell says. Sr. Gayhe took her p.m. to-day & I was quite busy. Spent my morning writing home & Len & Grace. There was a party to-night for us. & Mrs. Phips entertained c̄ her songs & delightful little Southern songs. She was very sweet & pretty. Had most of my packing to do tonight. & am so tired.

18 FRIDAY [49-317]

On duty till 11.30. Such a time saying good bye. The patients hate changes in the nursing staff. We went to the Stn. in an ambulance, & Miss Brand & Lill. I spent most of the pm. in London getting the luggage transferred etc. Lill & I had dinner c̄ Grace & Willie & got to the Kingsley at bed time. I sent a wire to Len, but hardly expect to see him. Lill bought a lovely writing case. Guess I'm taking a cold.

19 SATURDAY [50-316]

Off at 9.15. Victoria Stn. The ride to Folkstone is very pretty & it was a beautiful day. We went through the hop country, which is quite extensive. We passed right through Westenhanger, but it was too unexpected for me to keep a look out. The wind came up directly we got on board but the crossing was pretty smooth. One or two sick. Had lunch at the Louvre & got to camp about 4 p.m.

20 Septuagesima SUN [51-315]

Clare & I went for a nice walk to Napoleon's monument in the a.m. It is quite cold & windy. On duty in the p.m. in K 1 c̄ Miss MacIntosh & Samson & Gillen [illegible] quite busy. 3 huts c̄ 25 patients each. [illegible] tells me that Aunt Emma is dead.

Ruth's written entries from February.

FRIDAY, MARCH 3

A year ago today we went to Quebec. A convoy of ninety-six last night. My ward is quite filled so I had a busy day. Latest sensation: Miss Lamont[18] is resigning from the CAMC to be married. We are all taking heart, and Watling appeared among us again on the strength of it. Had a long talk with a 2nd C.M.R. today and am so glad to know that the 6th were not in the fuss of a short time ago. The O.C. of the 5th is in prison in England. Another rainy day with some hail and lots of wind. I put up some shelves today. Such a nice letter from Mrs. Sutherland tonight. A convoy of ninety-six last night.

SATURDAY, MARCH 4

A busy day. Evacuation to England and to Convalescent Camp. I sent some nice Canadians to "blighty." Had last hours and went to the "Revue" at Convalescent Camp. A splendid performance in every way. Well staged and cleverly played. It was a good clean laugh all through. Miss Toole and Miss Drake are with us again. Lill and I had tea with Watling in the hut after concert and we talked shop. A windy stormy day. Another shelf up today.

SUNDAY, MARCH 5

Clare and I went for a short walk this afternoon. The sun was shining and it was very spring like, the birds were singing and the brooks overflowing. It will be lovely here in the summer. A convoy of 100 last night. A year ago today we went to Quebec.[19]

MONDAY, MARCH 6

No entry

TUESDAY, MARCH 7

No entry

WEDNESDAY, MARCH 8

A convoy of 107, which arrived while the concert given by the Convalescent Camp party was in progress. Trench feet were most of the cases. The men bring stories that the Germans before vacating the trenches taken by us leave quantities of saltpetre, which accounts for the feet conditions. It is surely diabolical. Clare and I shopped in our p.m. off and arranged for French lessons. It remains to be seen what progress is made. Bought teaspoons and bread knife and sugar and salt.

THURSDAY, MARCH 9

A large convoy of 108. Mostly trench feet came in last night.

FRIDAY, MARCH 10

Another convoy of forty last night. The weather is improving today but still raining.

SATURDAY, MARCH 11

No entry

SUNDAY, MARCH 12

Quite a busy day. Clare and I went to No. 14 to see Miss MacNaughton and Brand. They are very nicely situated and well taken care of. Miss MacNaughton is to be operated on tomorrow. A large evacuation this evening.

MONDAY, MARCH 13

A small convoy of twenty last night. None came to us. It is summer weather today with some rain tonight. I feel as though I am getting another dose of cold, and I feel wretched.

TUESDAY, MARCH 14

I heard quite a bit of exciting news today that "Army"[20] and Cpt. Dixon[21] had been married before we left Canada. I am not altogether surprised. "Army" isn't feeling well and is resigning from the CAMC and will go home. A lovely day again. A good sized convoy last night with eleven new patients for us. All in K1. Had last hours and went for a short walk by myself.

WEDNESDAY, MARCH 15

Still another balmy, beautiful day. I had last hours. Clare and I went strolling after dinner. It was so lovely, and I visited Miss Cooper before going to bed. No convoy last night and the hospital is very light. No home mail yet. We will soon forget to look for any. Miss Sampson was sent to ward A this a.m.

THURSDAY, MARCH 16

A convoy of eighty odd last night. Six came to Miss Sampson's hut. One Canadian, Davidson from Sussex Ave., Montreal. Another beautiful day. We saw quite a number of airships today. Miss Cooper had a letter from Tuckie, who has her appointment at last. Like us she longs for home news. Has had no home letters since crossing. Miss MacIntosh is on night duty. Louise McLeod came to us after lunch. Miss Sampson is still in "A."

FRIDAY, MARCH 17

No entry

SATURDAY, MARCH 18

No entry

SUNDAY, MARCH 19

A beautiful day and I feel like the deuce.[22]

MONDAY, MARCH 20

A small convoy of forty odd came last night. Another lovely day but rather enervating. Had last hours and went in the "valley" with Stevie. It was better than moping in my room alone, though I feel very miserable with my throat.

TUESDAY, MARCH 21

Another convoy last night of seventy something. We got eight. Miss Sampson is with us again today. A rainy and rather cold day. There is a Princess Victoria concert this p.m. for the patients; repeated tonight for us. I stay at . . . . .[23]

WEDNESDAY, MARCH 22

No entry

THURSDAY, MARCH 23

Took my p.m. and spent it in bed.

FRIDAY, MARCH 24

A new addition to my cold, namely sore eyes. Have been called "pink eye" all day. A nice day but blowing.

SATURDAY, MARCH 25

Had letters from Bevan who is still in hospital and from Stephens who is at his home in Northumberland. Had Captain MacMillan look at my eyes, and he cauterized them with silver nitrate. Drastic treatment but they feel better already.

SUNDAY, MARCH 26

Wrote home, Len, also to Bevan and Stephens. Spent my time off visiting Nellie Tate who is quite miserable.

MONDAY, MARCH 27

On duty in the supply room with Naomi Gray and Miss Carpenter. Fairly bright in the a.m. but very windy and stormy in the afternoon. No mail tonight. Naomi and I walked in the valley in our hours off. Col. McRae goes to Paris on leave today.

TUESDAY, MARCH 28

Made rubber pillowcases all day. Naomi Gray goes on night duty tonight. A letter from Ray today. They are having cold weather at home. It is blowing a furious gale here and very cold. A convoy of sixty something this afternoon. We have taken some trenches I hear. My eyes are still very blurred and feel rather sore. Col. Elder's daughter Allison has died. A cable came today.

WEDNESDAY, MARCH 29

Col. Elder has gone home. So today's order says. It seems too bad he did not go a week ago. I am back in "K" again. Sampson,[24] Margery Ross,[25] and Jessie Sedgewick go on leave today but did not get off yet as there wasn't a boat.

THURSDAY, MARCH 30

Clare and Dickie's and my p.m. and such a wonderful afternoon for Clare. As we went out the gate her brother Cyril came in. He was on his way to England on furlong. It was such a fortunate meeting. He is like Clare in looks somewhat and in actions somewhat, but not in speech. We ate together in town and saw him to his barracks at 6 p.m. and watched them march to the boat, then got our hair washed and came home, tired but happy. The girls go off at last today.

FRIDAY, MARCH 31

Another fine day. Had last hours. Clare and I walked a new way to Wimereux and back by the valley. Such a beautiful country. Had letters from Helen Donald, Ray, and one from Pen Robertson. Lapp's substitute arrived in camp today, but Lapp is still with us. We will miss him when he goes.

In April, the weather improves quickly and with it come spring flowers, including the planting of transplants outside the ward huts by recovering patients. This gives them something to do, improves morale, and makes the bleak camp less depressing. On the seventh, Clare's younger brother Cyril visits on his way back "up the line." Fortunately, both Ruth and Clare have their half day off and can treat the boys to a nice meal out. Ruth relates that they ate "in town." This is not just because the food is good, but in truth they had no other choice. Clare and Ruth are officers, and enlisted men and officers cannot "mess" together on army property. The war, however, is coming ever closer to the McGill Unit. On the sixteenth, Ruth records the first sighting of a German airplane. This one drops a bomb, the commencement of a very dangerous and deadly trend.

Despite earlier treatment, Ruth's eyes continue to bother her, and a few days later it becomes clear why. Ruth has contracted the measles. She is immediately removed from No. 3 CGH and, in accord with army procedure, placed in quarantine at No. 14 British General Hospital. She will remain there until May 6. Her fellow nurses send her flowers and visit. Clare visits her twice and records in her diary on the twenty-sixth that

"Miss Brand and I walked out to the Isolation Hospital at Wimereux this morning and talked with Ruth through her little hut door. She is better and will get up today."[26] Another visitor is Colonel John McRae, who visits Ruth on May 5. Ruth appreciates the visits, but clearly the theory and practice of isolation is taken very seriously. Contagious diseases have to be contained–the war effort demands it.

SATURDAY, APRIL 1

A beautiful day but cold tonight. Had last hours and did nothing. Edith Leslie is on night duty. Reta and Wrights and Jane and Connie had lunch with us in our room tonight. The "Fall in" has just gone. Sent sixteen men to C.C.[27] today. A year ago I went home from Quebec.

SUNDAY, APRIL 2

A busy day on the ward. Chalmers Salter called to see me today. He is in a cycle corps and has been down at a rest camp. He looks well and every inch a Salter.

MONDAY, APRIL 3

A glorious day and garden making goes on merrily. Had last hours and wrote home.

TUESDAY, APRIL 4

No entry

WEDNESDAY, APRIL 5

No entry

THURSDAY, APRIL 6

Individual gardens are in the making in front of the different huts, the patients are the gardeners. The days are fine and great growing weather.

FRIDAY, APRIL 7

I had my p.m. and Clare expected to have hers too, and Cyril came on his way from leave. Such good luck. A Nova Scotian boy was with him, and I took the N.S. boy with me so Clare could have Cyril to herself. He looks rested and very fit again. We ate in town and saw the boys to their train and then visited the bookstore and had a nice time generally. Found a letter from Len on our return. He is doing some extra shooting these days. A convoy of sixty-seven came in this p.m. All Canadians and a great many 27th Battalion men.

SATURDAY, APRIL 8

Off 2–4 and finished covering my chair, a work which has been going on for some time. We can hear some firing and explosions tonight. Clare and I read the Freelands[28] this evening, but as usual got sidetracked in a discussion. The Queen's girls[29] (ten of them) arrived tonight to be here till their unit locates again. The girls are back from leave tonight.

SUNDAY, APRIL 9

A small convoy last night. Off last hours. A beautiful day but turned cold and dark in the late afternoon. Mrs. Douglas[30] has been giving me an account of their doings in the East.

MONDAY, APRIL 10

A very lovely day but my feet are sore again. Mrs. Cooper and Clare and I went plant hunting before dinner. The "Fall in" has just gone again, which means "convoy."

TUESDAY, APRIL 11

The convoy wasn't large—around forty, I think. We got a few, three nice 21st Battalion men among them. They seem like old friends. Our extra Sisters are not Queen's but No. 3 Stationary composed of Contingent nurses with the exception of Mrs. Douglas who was transferred from Queen's. They are very nice girls.

WEDNESDAY, APRIL 12

Miss Whitney had her p.m. and I took morning hours. Miss Cooper and I went down to the market in the rain. Miss Cooper bought plants for the gardens, and we had a fine time. I of course was soaked, but it was a nice outing. Such a wild stormy day. Bought some of those nice coconut biscuits.

THURSDAY, APRIL 13

Lou Gillis had her afternoon, and Miss Whitney went to a concert downtown with the patients from our line, so we had a busy day. Had a nice long letter from Laura today. She is busy teaching, housekeeping, etc. A nice bright day, rather breezy. Mrs. Douglas visited us tonight and told us of their experiences and trials while in Lemnos.

FRIDAY, APRIL 14

Clare and I had our afternoon, and we went to Le Portel and Outreau, going to Le Portel by train from Boulogne and walking back via Outreau. It was a windy, showery day and neither of us were in good trim. I had a headache and we were very mopey. The church (where we took shelter during a shower) is very ugly, but there is fresh French girls with such quaint bonnets at work there cleaning. We shopped on our way home. A concert by Mrs. Lake Hope and party in the evening, an excellent entertainment but my headache unbearable. Evacuation to England today.

SATURDAY, APRIL 15

A windy day again but bright at intervals with rain showers occasionally A busy day in K and two hemorrhages. Whitney spent her day there, and I had last hours. The convoy was so odd last night, mostly British and some bad cases. An evacuation to England this a.m.

SUNDAY, APRIL 16

A German airship gave us some excitement this a.m. A bomb was dropped not far from here, but no damage as far as we know. The French anti guns gave them a lively time, and some shrapnel from them struck one of the patients. Clare and I spent our hours off in the citadel. A nice day but cool.

MONDAY, APRIL 17

Rather a wild day with high wind and some rain. A convoy last night with bad cases. We got a burn case. Churchill from Yarmouth, NS, a lobster fisherman.[31] Alice Stewart's brother admitted, not much hurt. Miss Steel and Miss Lindsay leave us today for Le Tréport. Our unit is changing. This is six gone. I wrote to Jessie Fowler.

TUESDAY, APRIL 18

Miss Starke was taken to No. 14 this a.m., and Louise McGreer went on special leave to Paris to be with her brother at their aunt's. Another wild day. Watling is in the O.R. in Louise's absence. Had a letter from Helen and one from Len.

WEDNESDAY, APRIL 19

Went to Capt. MacMillan's and had my eye cauterized again and took my p.m. to nurse it. Spent the afternoon in bed and Clare read to me. Dickie and Watling went into town. A French Opera Company gave a concert here tonight and the girls attended.

THURSDAY, APRIL 20

Wrote a couple of letters for patients and also to R. and C. for collars. A rough showery day with lots of wind. My eyes are better and I feel more cheerful.

FRIDAY, APRIL 21

No entry

SATURDAY, APRIL 22

Eyes worse than ever. Capt. MacMillan cauterized them at noon and sent me off duty with black glasses and orders not to read or write.

APRIL 23, EASTER SUNDAY

This entry written May 8. Ruth came down with the measles and wrote the entries of April 23 to April 28 as best she could remember after she recovered. Daily entries begin again April 29.

Rather miserable, I remember. Clare and Stevie and I took our tea and Kipling to the valley and Clare read to me in the evening.

MONDAY, APRIL 24

Was covered with measles when I wakened, and in two hours was in an ambulance on my way to No. 14 Stationary Hospital. Felt very miserable and ashamed of myself and so glad to stay in bed.

APRIL 25, EASTER TUESDAY

"and the evening and the morning were the 1st day." Dickie and Watling and Reta Pole sent me beautiful red roses, and they did me a world of good. Had a nice Scotch nurse, Miss Coulter, and an Australian sister who disarranged my room to perfection. Capt. Gaunt is M.O.—English and an old Army man, having been in Malta for the outbreak of war.

WEDNESDAY, APRIL 26

The spots began to fade, though bed was still nice. I think I mailed a card to Lill this day for clothes. More sick nurses in.

THURSDAY, APRIL 27

I think I got my clothes this day. Matron and Mrs. Hoerner[32] bringing them, and Dickie and Naomi Gray came to see me later in the day.

FRIDAY, APRIL 28

Got up for a short time and glad to go back to bed again I remember.

SATURDAY, APRIL 29

I am to go home on the third. My tenth day. Up all day today. Had a visit from Clare and Brandie and the Padre belonging here. Had a letter from Len.

SUNDAY, APRIL 30

I walked to the beach and we had service in our own compound.

Ruth begins May still in hospital at No. 14 British General. She returns to No. 3 CGH on May 6. After two days' light duty in the supply room, she is switched to night duty for the next few weeks. At first, she specializes a very sick man by the name of Thomas, but once he begins to recover she is moved to the pneumonia tent. Ward P is a medical as opposed to a surgical ward, and Ruth is relieved and thankful for the change of pace and atmosphere. The month also sees Ruth and Clare rent new bicycles and return to their roving ways. However, roving about on bikes is not what it used to be a few months earlier and now requires special permission passes. Their visit to Col. Birkett to ask for passes evokes some cynical comments from Ruth concerning "military" manners and efficiency. Nonetheless, they do obtain the required passes. Their travels include detours to see their nurse friend "Starkie" (also written as "Starkney") who is, unfortunately, very ill at No. 14 British General. Finally, Ruth's night duties end on the twenty-ninth, and two days later she, along with Dickie and Watling, begins a two-week leave to England.

MONDAY, MAY 1

No entry

TUESDAY, MAY 2

No entry

Ruth during an introspective moment in France.

WEDNESDAY, MAY 3

My tenth day but discovered that I was not to get off home till Thursday. Clare down to see me in the a.m.

THURSDAY, MAY 4

No entry

FRIDAY, MAY 5

Had a visit from Col. McRae in the afternoon, and Miss Walker and Miss Sommer and I went for a long walk on the shore. I would enjoy another day here. A letter from Len. They are moving again to Dibgate, which makes their fifth move in a year.

SATURDAY, MAY 6

Winnie Brown[33] and Miss Hobkirk[34] came to see me with Clare and Lill in the a.m. Was discharged from hospital and came home at 3 p.m. bringing Miss Coulter with me to tea and dinner. An anniversary dance in the evening. One year today since we sailed from Montreal.

SUNDAY, MAY 7

On duty in the supply room and relieving in the wards if necessary. Had last hours.

MONDAY, MAY 8

In supply room and equipping wards R1 and 3 in a.m. Off duty at 2 p.m. to go on night duty and specializing a convulsion case in H. Such a night. Patient had twenty-two convulsions during my duty hours and is still holding his own this a.m. (Tuesday 9th). A convoy last night.

TUESDAY, MAY 9

On duty with Thomas again. Just two convulsions today and he looks better. No definite diagnosis yet. I had a good sleep today. Lill is in R tonight. Miss Grere in D, Reta Pole in L.

WEDNESDAY, MAY 10

Thomas had a hemorrhage last night and was not so well this a.m. The nights are dreary and I spent the whole day sleeping. There was a convoy last night—sixty something.

THURSDAY, MAY 11

My patient had a good night and day and is better. Had a letter from Len and Ray. Len's OC is talking about giving Len a musketry course. Len is still longing to get to France. Kerr is doing well but I haven't seen him since I came on night duty. Frances MacKeen[35] is off with neuralgia today. I am taking tonsillitis and just loaded with rheumatism.

FRIDAY, MAY 12

Thomas is just fine and does not need me. An orderly is more to the purpose, and I have just told Capt. Reford so. Had a letter from Miss Walker today. She had the week off. So was much more fortunate than I. The tonsillitis is such a thing and I did not sleep today. A convoy of fifty tonight. Wrote to Leonard.

SATURDAY, MAY 13

A stormy day and cold tonight. Am on with Thomas again and have an orderly. A letter from H. Morrison today and a "World." Edith Stewart came back last night and we have a VAD[36]—Miss Ross from Westmount. A very pretty girl. Took her training in England and is assisting the Home Sisters[37] here. She does not wear buttons or stars.

SUNDAY, MAY 14

Got a box of sweets from Laura tonight. Wrote home. Am specializing a C.S. case in H3 tonight. A convoy of seventy is in. A cold wet night.

MONDAY, MAY 15

On duty in the pneumonia tent tonight. Four patients, one very ill, a 21st boy, Cpl. Jones, a friend of Bert Gourley's and Miss Bliss's. A cold night but fine and bright moonlight. Babbitt and Lill and I went into town this a.m. I got some money to pay my bills. We are terribly worried about Starkney. The girls who have seen her say she is very ill indeed.

TUESDAY, MAY 16

In Ward P and so glad to be in a medical instead of a surgical ward. No very sick men. The orderlies change tonight and mine did not show up. A cold night with heavy fog towards morning. A convoy last night. Not receiving.

WEDNESDAY, MAY 17

It has been a beautiful day. Clare went to market this a.m. I straight to bed and slept till the afternoon. A bright fine night, so still and quiet. Ward P not receiving. Report says Starkie very ill.

THURSDAY, MAY 18

Clare and I went down town, and Clare bought a bicycle and I ordered one like it. Got some vases to send to No. 14 and bought a French enamel trinket box for Helen. Am feeling so much better and am having an easy night duty.

FRIDAY, MAY 19

A letter from home today. A beautiful warm day. Clare and Connie went walking this a.m. I went to bed.

SATURDAY, MAY 20

Clare and I wheeled to Boulogne and had some changes made in Clare's wheel. Pedals changed and another seat substituted. I got my hair washed. Another beautiful day and the world looks lovely.

SUNDAY, MAY 21

Clare and I went to Col. Birkett to ask for passes and were received in true military style and were given military satisfaction. We have an idea he doesn't intend us to have them at all. A German airship overhead today with the usual gun firing. A very beautiful day. Wrote home last night and mailed a package—"Fragments from France" and Helen's trinket box.

MONDAY, MAY 22

Clare and I were to go to No. 14 this afternoon, but it rained. It is a sullen night. A convoy of forty is in. Wrote Laura this evening and had letter from Rae and Leonard. Len tells me he is to go for leave in June and is going to Scotland.

TUESDAY, MAY 23

Clare and I went bicycling. Called at No. 14 and saw Miss Coulter and Miss Gordon and Capt. Gaunt and left the vases behind. Saw Starkie for a few minutes. She looks much better and is progressing satisfactorily. We wheeled on down almost to Ambleteuse and then turned inland and came home by way of Wimille and the valley. We reported to the Col. this p.m. and got our passes. So that little difficulty is over. It is a cold night. We received, but no word of a convoy.

WEDNESDAY, MAY 24

Clare and I went down to the Valley for breakfast. We enjoyed it but will not repeat, as the food is not very good and not overly clean. The morning was lovely and the arbours are very nice. A convoy tonight and I got eleven. One 21st boy who has been very ill up the line. Mrs. Mann got word this a.m. (25th) that her father is dead. I have just been to see her.

THURSDAY, MAY 25

Warrie Loggie came today on his way to England and visited an hour. He looks well but much older. Was able to give him Kerr's address in Birmingham. Clare and Connie left for Hardelot this a.m. but the barrier sergeant (English) would not accept the passes for the bicycles. Clare went to the P.A.O.[38] and Connie came home. A cold night and orders for all lights out. A spy was caught down town today, and a Zepp raid is suspected. More guns heard today. Wrote Rae and a note to Winnie Brown. Warrie says Walter is wounded.

FRIDAY, MAY 26

Slept all day. Another cold night and a small convoy in. We are not receiving. Mrs. Forgey heard today that her mother has died. Miss Bliss relieved her till 9 p.m. I feel so sorry for her. Clare is back after a rather disappointing holiday alone. She went to Hardelot in the car, leaving the bicycle in Boulogne. The passes were signed by the A.P.M.[39] but are not the regular thing and rather doubtful.

SATURDAY, MAY 27

We are to go on leave next Tuesday. Have written Len to see if we can make a connection. Wrote Grace and Mrs. Walker last night and Clare Harrington tonight. Eleven local cases in today. Two very sick men. R's quarantined tonight. Lill is off duty.

SUNDAY, MAY 28

A letter from Murray tonight. Walter is in hospital somewhere.

MONDAY, MAY 29

I am off night duty and we go for leave tomorrow. Slept in the a.m. and went down to Boulogne with Watling and Louise McGreer at 3 o'clock. Got my hair washed and bought a nightgown and corset cover. Clare met me and we called about our bicycles. Mine not finished yet.

TUESDAY, MAY 30

We crossed at 10:20—a smooth trip. Len did not show up, and we had to wait for a second train and book seats ahead. There was such a crush of leave people bunched on the train and came to the Cecil. Went to see "Romance" at the Lysie. I didn't care much for it.

WEDNESDAY, MAY 31

Met Mrs. Nichols on the street this a.m. She is waiting for her ticket home for a two months' leave. She looked very smart in her mufti. In the p.m. we went to Grace's for tea and saw Tini at the Adolphi in the evening. It was rather pretty but not much plot and no good acting.

Ruth is on leave in London as the month begins and, fortunately, her brother Len is able to come up from his camp in the south of England to join her. After a few days, Ruth and her friends leave London for an extensive tour of Scotland, but the war is never far away. While in Edinburgh, their aid is commandeered to assist in the off-loading of a train of wounded soldiers. They also learn of the violent death at sea of Lord Kitchener, who drowned when his ship struck a German mine. This is a major blow to the Empire's war morale. Kitchener is admired and greatly respected, and it is his image on the famous recruiting posters. Finally, upon returning to London, Ruth learns, in a letter from Clare, of her cousin Murray Anderson's wounding during the bloody battle of Mount Sorrel. Clare's brother Cyril is also a casualty and will lose his foot as a result.

Soon after her return to No. 3 GCH, Ruth begins a ten-day night shift duty on the seventeenth. In the mornings she bicycles, eats rabbit pie and pancakes, writes her brother Len and cousin Murray, and, along with Clare, starts French language lessons. There is, however, an ominous sign–despite fairly heavy casualties arriving at No. 3 CGH, orders are received to clear them out as quickly as possible. The reason for this will become clear in the first week of July as the massive battle of the Somme begins.

THURSDAY, JUNE 1

Len arrived as we were going out and he spent the day with us. We lunched at the Station where we were booking berths for Edinburgh and had tea at the Army and Navy where Lill and I bought raincoats. In between we made mistakes in buses and shopped. A new experience for Len. I got a hat and sweater. Watling shopped for the girls. Dinner at the Cecil and to the train at 10:30 p.m.

FRIDAY, JUNE 2

Got to Edinburgh at 8:30 and put up at the Balmoral on Princess St. and spent the day sightseeing. A jolly old veteran showed us the wonders of Calton Hill, and then we walked down the Canongate to Holyrood, which was unfortunately closed until the tenth on account of the Lord High Commissioner's visit. Then we visited St. Giles, which has a Thistle Chapel attached now and most exquisite bit of oak carving. In the p.m. we went to the Castle and had a half-seasoner guide to show us round.

SATURDAY, JUNE 3

Came up to Inverness on the ten train. Had a lunch basket at Kingruisse and were ready for it. A chaplain on leave from the front travelled with us and was very interesting. Killecrankie and Drumossie are not half so grand viewed from the train as from a motor. Are stopping at the Station Hotel. I had a headache and went straight to bed.

SUNDAY, JUNE 4

Church in the a.m. at a U.F.[40] and a motor drive out to Culloden Moor after lunch and then tea in the lounge and church again in the evening. An old-fashioned one this time with a presenter and no organ. A good preacher and a full church of MacDonalds and Monroes and Frasers, etc. Good homey folk.

MONDAY, JUNE 5

Col. Moise commandeered us last night to help with a train of wounded soldiers. There was just thirty of them. I went up to the Infirmary with an officer terribly burned about the face and hands. The girls walked up and helped with drinks. All the cases were burns and scalds. We came down to Edinburgh on the 3:50 in company with an officer and his wife from HMS *Malaya*. Edinburgh looks lovely and the Balmoral seems like home after the Station Hotel at Inverness. We had supper in our room before a nice fire. Luxury. Will we ever be able to work again? I bought a trinket box and picture frame and sent a mustard pot to Mrs. Edmonds and Lill, and I sent a pepper one to Mrs. Greig. I mailed the 1st HT & Private Lawson to Dad.

TUESDAY, JUNE 6

We taxied around the Queen's Drive and in the afternoon went out to Roslyn Castle. Everyone is stunned with the news of Lord Kitchener's death. The guide to the chapel could scarcely get through his lesson, his mind was so upset. Roslyn Chapel is wonderful and exquisite and the castle is well worth revisiting. It has been a blowy day. The newsboys are doing a rushing business yet with extras. We leave tomorrow for the Trossachs trip.

WEDNESDAY, JUNE 7

An early start 9 a.m. Changed at Sterling and again at Buchlyvie. Lunch at Aberfoyle and then coach to Loch Catrine. The boat trip was cold and it rained at intervals. Coach again for Stronachlacher to Inversnaid, tea there and boat down Loch Lomand to Balloch's. The trip is nice but not to be compared to the Caladonia Canal. Got to Glasgow in time for dinner. Tarbot looked very nice and Loch Lomand is by far the prettiest loch of the group. Am at the Queens St. Station.

THURSDAY, JUNE 8

Breakfast in bed and up about eleven. The girls went out to a hospital to see Johnnie Baird's sister who is in training there, and I went to the Donalds for tea and stayed until nine. It has rained at intervals most of the day.

FRIDAY, JUNE 9

Breakfast up this a.m. Shopped till lunch and then went to the Cathedral. I mailed an old snuff box to Papa, a "Kidnapped" and "The Master of Ballentrie" and bought some new ones. Miss Donald came in for a few minutes before prepositorie[41] service, and Mrs. Donald gave us a call. Princess Louise and Prince Louis of Battenberg are guests at the hotel banquet tonight. We leave on the 10:20 tonight.

SATURDAY, JUNE 10

Nearly lunch time when we reached London, and the shops close at one o'clock. I got shoes but have to go back without all the other necessaries. A letter from Len and two from Clare, telling me that Murray is wounded. The Canadian casualties have been terrible. I phoned the Canadian Red Cross and the Record office, but neither Murray nor Walter's names are on the list.

SUNDAY, JUNE 11

Breakfast in bed and I wrote letters home, Murray, Miss Leduc, Len, and Walter. We spent the day in the hotel.

MONDAY, JUNE 12

Find on arriving at Folkstone that we cannot cross till evening. I bought a bicycle and motored out to Dibgate to find Len gone to a lecture and Capt. MacNaughton[42] out of camp. It was a rainy disagreeable p.m. and spent the extra time in the hotel near the boat. The crossing was smooth. The Victoria Concert party came over with us. I saw Len and Art Allen for a few minutes and Jim MacNaughton came on board. He looks very well. The 55th are attached to the 23rd for the time being. Jim does not think there is much chance for Len to get over just now. We got up from the boat with Capt. Little,[43] who had the car.

TUESDAY, JUNE 13

Am in Ward R reopening after Isolation. Bert Gourley and Miss Harrsion's brothers are patients here. Louise McGreer's brother is killed, and Mrs. Griffin is afraid for Alex. I wrote Len enclosing £1 for him to cable Uncle Will. Found a letter from Murray and Walter. Murray's at Le Tréport, Walter is ok but is very nervous I hear. Found letters from Aunt Janet and two from Ray and one from John Shaw.

WEDNESDAY, JUNE 14

In S today with a few patients. I am to do my ten days' night duty with my next turn. The hospital is light, evacuating everything as it comes in, if possible.

THURSDAY, JUNE 15

A large convoy last night and fifty-eight new patients in S with no surgical equipment to work with. Miss Clark[44] with me and we had a busy day. No hours.

FRIDAY, JUNE 16

Miss Green came to see us today so we had a light day. Miss Clark took her p.m. off. Through poor management on the M.O.'s part, the work is extended through the entire day.

SATURDAY, JUNE 17

I had my p.m. today. Another convoy last night but S not receiving.

SUNDAY, JUNE 18

Clare and Stevie and I wheeled to Souverain Moulin and had dinner there. Rabbit pie and pancakes for which the place is famous. A lovely ride and a very pleasant time.

MONDAY, JUNE 19– FRIDAY, JUNE 23

No entries

SATURDAY, JUNE 24

Still no letter from Len and no Canadian mail.

SUNDAY, JUNE 25

Off last hours. Clare and I took our tea and wheeled into the country. We watched the village procession at Baincthun, it being Corpus Christi. I got a beautiful puncture, and we had to walk home after eating our tea and entertaining two French maidens.

MONDAY, JUNE 26

Off for long hours 1–4 and did a little cleaning up. Have spent the evening with Clare who made a "verbal will" in view of possible demise while on leave. I started a letter home today. Dennie Gould[45] is in O. I met Fred there this evening. Miss Coulter has gone up the lines. Naomi was at No. 14 to see a patient today.

TUESDAY, JUNE 27

Showery but pleasant. A small convoy last night. S not receiving. The Col. etc. made official rounds this p.m. I hope it will do MacKenzie good. Clare and I had a French lesson. Such a trial for me. My brain is in a whirl.

WEDNESDAY, JUNE 28

Letter from Ray and Miss Richardson. Helen Donald and Isabel MacNaughton have young daughters. I wrote Isabel and Miss Richardson this p.m. Early hours and Clare and I studied French.

THURSDAY, JUNE 29

Morning hours. Miss C has her p.m. Clare slept in. Wrote Miss Ledoux and Warrie L. and began one to Helen Donald. Letters from Len and Murray tonight. Murray is in hospital in Netley[46] and does not like it. He still has his shrapnel. Len sent the cable, I am glad to hear. He is talking of parading to get clear of going to a new reserve corp. being formed. I wrote him and Murray tonight.

FRIDAY, JUNE 30

Last hours. I fixed Nicholas Nickelby and Great Expectations for mailing tomorrow. Mail has arrived at last but all old letters.

July 1, 1916, marks the beginning of the Battle of the Somme–one of the longest and costliest battles of the Great War. Initial British and Australian casualties are horrendous. Ruth and everyone else at No. 3 CGH will experience a hitherto unprecedented rush of men with ghastly wounds. Ruth records some of the numbers: 600 new cases on July 7; 836 new admissions on July 10, with 1,100 wounded soldiers discharged still leaving 1,112 patients in the hospital. Finally, on July 21, 615 admissions, 421 discharges, and 1,039 passing through their Admissions and Discharge department–cases assessed but not admitted. These men are sufficiently stable to be able to be sent "down the line" to England by boat.

On the third, Ruth mentions three nurses sent forward to Casualty Clearing Stations, and on the eighth Clare references the hospital as being nine nurses short.47 In the midst of all this the nurses see a need and volunteer to take on an extra task in their off hours. As the stretcher bearers and orderlies are literally working around the clock with no breaks, not even to eat, a canteen is created to provide them with food. This Red Cross canteen also provides a hot drink and a sandwich to the wounded soldiers who can walk to it. The busyness and stress of the month, as well as Ruth's recurring headaches, explain the five days of missing entries. Ruth almost forgets her birthday on the eighteenth, but her good friend Clare did not. She gives Ruth a tiny Joan of Arc pendant. Clare clearly realizes that even in the midst of such tragedy, it is important to mark life's milestones. Ruth is now thirty-three.

SATURDAY, JULY 1

There was an impromptu concert in the new Red Cross hut. Capt. Harrison presiding. It wasn't too bad for all it was a family affair. Clare gave two recitations. Well given as usual. Went to the cemetery in the a.m. to decorate the Canadian graves of which there are hundreds. I took my full day off, which has been coming to me for a long time.

SUNDAY, JULY 2

Clare and I wheeled to Wirwignes and had tea in the Boulogne woods. Such a lovely tea too.

MONDAY, JULY 3

Convoys are frequent and large and evacuation rapid. Clare and I went down to see Miss Drake at No. 14. We had morning hours and we lunched in Wimereux. Miss Glendenning and

Miss Fortescue[48] went up to a clearing Hospital tonight. That makes three more off our staff.

TUESDAY, JULY 4

Clare and Alice Stewart went to Convalescent Camp today to do dressings there. A canteen has been instituted to last through the rush. Object—to provide the men on stretchers etc. with a hot drink and something palatable to eat. Coffee and cocoa and egg and salmon and sardine sandwiches. The pathological to the site and the food provided by the hospital and a fund through Capt. Little. The work is entirely voluntary on the sisters' part.

WEDNESDAY, JULY 5

The wards are extremely busy and the khaki is kept in the wards. Consequently we are walking away.[49] S2 is no sight for the Gods. Clare and I wheeled down to No. 14 to see Mrs. Drake after dinner. She is much better. Leaves are off. She and Clare can't get away for some time.

THURSDAY, JULY 6

Lill went walking in the valley with the Matron this evening. I did another bit of volunteer work.
Everybody is busy and there are frequently overflow from the hospital dumped in on us till next boat time.

FRIDAY, JULY 7

Over 600 came to us last night. We are still with just one orderly. Am so thankful my feet are not sore. We had thirty-six stretcher cases in S2 for overnight. They were from the hospital at Camiers and Étaples and arrived too late for their boat. We get no credit on our lists for these extras.

SATURDAY, JULY 8

Report has that our hospital has been complimented by the D.D.M.S.[50] for efficiency during this big rush. Certainly everyone has worked well, even Williams. Reports from the patients seem good. They are mostly from Albert-Tricourt and Boisselle.

SUNDAY, JULY 9

Clare and Alice Stewart are still at C.C. And our hospital needs them badly.

MONDAY, JULY 10

Large convoys all night and everyone is very busy. This is a record for twenty-four hours; 836 cases admitted and 1,100 discharged with 1,112 remaining at 6 p.m.

TUESDAY, JULY 11

More convoy and a sick headache. A whole ward of Australians last night. Very few Blighty cases this time.

WEDNESDAY, JULY 12

No entry

THURSDAY, JULY 13

Clare and I were on canteen tonight and it was well patronized. Stevie and K. MacLeod[51] assisted. No headache today.

FRIDAY, JULY 14

Headache day with interest.

SATURDAY, JULY 15

There is a little party tonight for Sal Chisholm. Clare and I went for a short ride, but I feel so miserable that there isn't much pleasure.

SUNDAY, JULY 15

Miss Chisholm left today for England. She is to be married shortly.

MONDAY, JULY 17

Another headache. The days off are getting fewer.

TUESDAY, JULY 18

My birthday—I suddenly realized as I made out the diet sheet. Clare and I went for a ride tonight, and she gave me a wee Joan of Arc pendant. A dear little one and Clare is so thoughtful. I feel much less grumpy but wish I had never <u>begun</u> French. It takes too much time.

WEDNESDAY, JULY 19

Headache day again.

THURSDAY, JULY 20

War news from the Somme district still continues good. Three convoys last night.

FRIDAY, JULY 21

Terrific explosions of some sort went on all night and this a.m. Something has happened somewhere.[52] The men seem to think it is on land. Our windows rattled and the huts shook. More convoys last night and the canteen was well patronized.
Admissions today: 615
Discharges: 421
Passed through A&D[53] Room: 1,039

SATURDAY, JULY 22

We hear for a certainty today that the Germans got 26,000 tons of ammunition last night. They dropped bombs on our largest ammunition supply base, and one explosion followed another all night and forenoon. The base is a short distance inland from Calais, and the village was practically destroyed and a number of casualties. This will not get into the papers no doubt.

SUNDAY, JULY 23

Clare and I bicycled after dinner to Souverin Moulin. We had coffee and cake and came home by Wimille through the Valley. Rain stopped us from going on to Wierre-Effroy.

MONDAY, JULY 24

No entry

TUESDAY, JULY 25

No entry

WEDNESDAY, JULY 26

Queen Emilie of Portugal visited the hospital this afternoon, attended by Lady Gifford. Her Majesty took tea in our mess and made the rounds of the wards. Queen Emilie paid us a visit last year in Camiers.

THURSDAY, JULY 27

Half day. Lill and Clare and Reta Powell and Eva Bradley and I got a carriage and drove to Marquise by way of Ambleteuse, coming home by Souverin Moulin. Mr. Markham's concert party played "Which is Which." A letter from home tonight.

FRIDAY, JULY 28–SUNDAY, JULY 30

No entries

MONDAY, JULY 31

Had my inoculation this evening so that is over. I hope it doesn't make me sick. No letters tonight. Matron in Chief here today.

The Battle of the Somme continues to rage on. Ruth does not take her inoculation well–she feels sick for days. Unfortunately, the exact nature of this particular inoculation is not recorded on her medical file. (She received three needles for typhoid the previous year.) Not surprisingly, the stress of work, worries over her cousin Murray's wound, and the heat of the summer all conspire to give her recurring headaches. She finds some relief in occasional bike rides with Clare and by attending local events such as Boulogne's annual Marian festival on the twentieth. Her friend Clare goes on leave on the twenty-fifth and spends most of her time visiting her brother Cyril in hospital in England.[54] *The big news, however, is that Ruth has a male caller–Sunderland,*[55] *an Australian who was in her care at No. 3 CGH. Once he improved he was sent to the nearby Convalescent Camp, but he now returns to visit. He and Ruth go for a walk on the twenty seventh and stroll and dine together on the twenty-eighth. Typically, by the twenty-ninth he has to go "back up the line." Ruth is both concerned and saddened to see him go. As she confides to her diary, "He is an exceptionally nice boy and very interesting to me. So many things in common."*

TUESDAY, AUGUST 1

Clare insisted on going for the afternoon, and I remain off. I lay outside on Clare's couch and hugged my misery. A beautiful day, warm and bright.

WEDNESDAY, AUGUST 2

No entry

THURSDAY, AUGUST 3

I took early p.m. hours to get my French lesson in. Mademoiselle was late as usual. I never get a full lesson now, and I find them so difficult and require so much time.

FRIDAY, AUGUST 4

Heavy guns firing last night. This begins the third year of the war. I wonder what next August fourth will bring. Another beautiful day. A letter from Murray tonight. He has been operated on and is feeling better. The shrapnel must stay in it seems, and Murray will be incapacitated to a great extent. Poor Murray.

SATURDAY, AUGUST 5

Clare and I wheeled to Wierre-Effroy after first dinner. A lovely ride and the village is very pretty. We will go again when we have more time. Bicycle rides are few these days.

SUNDAY, AUGUST 6

And a splitting headache. Had last hours and went to bed and wept. Such a miserable world at times. A letter from Len tonight.

MONDAY, AUGUST 7

Still the remains of yesterday's headache. It's quite cool today. Got an announcement of Jean and Bryson's marriage. A rather worrisome day. Eight operations in the a.m. More gun firing somewhere today.

TUESDAY, AUGUST 8

A cool day. Wrote home and a card to Len and Murray and a letter to Johnston and studied a wee bit. Haven't much gumption for anything. Clare McLeod went to England today. She is to be married soon. King George is in Boulogne we hear and is to visit the hospitals.

WEDNESDAY, AUGUST 9

Off for early p.m. hours and tried to study but a headache threatened so I gave it up. My French lessons are a failure for want of study. Two should study together. Baxendale[56] has my bicycle this evening. Was posted for second inoculation but am to have it tomorrow instead. A patient gave me the eagle from a German helmet today. We evacuated and are full up again. More Australians. It has been a very warm day. Miss Clark had her p.m., and she and Naomi had tea in the Vallée.

THURSDAY, AUGUST 10

Miss Burt's half day. I had early p.m. hours, and Clare and I had a French lesson. More gun firing today. Got our postcards today and they were quite a success. Had a nice letter from home. The new roses are out and are lovely. Mrs. Holton is still with them and they are glad to have her. Had my second inoculation tonight. No headache today. How I would love to have at talk with Mama and Mrs. Holton on our veranda.

FRIDAY, AUGUST 11

Had my half day. Went down town with Naomi Gray and then to bed. Headache and temperature. Clare and Connie Stewart[57] and Corine MacKay[58] went for a bicycle picnic. Another hot day although it threatened rain in the a.m. Janet Rodd[59] is in bed today from her inoculation.

SATURDAY, AUGUST 12

Threatening rain again. We received a convoy of medicals. A letter from Murray tonight. He is at a Canadian Convalescent Camp in Hastings, Sussex, and likes it very much. My letters are not reaching him very quickly. Miss Stevens is here tonight visiting Myrtle. She is having midnight supper with her. Jane R. is still off duty. Got our snaps today.

SUNDAY, AUGUST 13

Miss Clark and I had last hours, and Clare and Naomi and Miss C. and I took our tea down to the valley. Clare and Naomi read "Her Majesty's Servants" out loud while the French boys presented Miss C. with ivy. I did nothing and enjoyed everything.

MONDAY, AUGUST 14

The Queen's men[60] are being recalled to their unit we hear. MacKenzie will go if the rumour is true. Threatening rain all day.

TUESDAY, AUGUST 15

Such a windy day. A letter or two from patients but no Canadian mail. A card from Rhodes and a letter from Lyburn.

WEDNESDAY, AUGUST 16

Miss Clark had her half day and went to Paris Plage. I went down with Clare to the bank and bought some stuff for the ward, and we got bread etc. for a picnic tomorrow. Letters from Ray and Miss Richardson and Laura who is in San Diego. Helen is running Sandie's motor.

THURSDAY, AUGUST 17

I had last hours and we had our picnic in the beautiful valley. Brandie read aloud "They" and "Below the Milldam."[61] Both severely criticized by the readers. Clare and I wheeling this evening back to Abbey Mallin, a lovely spot. We hope for a picnic there later on. Miss Clark is on night duty tonight.

FRIDAY, AUGUST 18

Cpl. Benger is ill and admitted to S today. Temp high and sore neck and back. We are keeping Cpl. Clark of the 6th F.A. in to help out in Benger's place. Stevie in with us today and Miss Brand is in Ward H, a convenient change as Brandie does not like Cpt. Loggie and Stevie does not like Cpt. Reford.

SATURDAY, AUGUST 19

My half day. Clare's too. We went down town for some things for Benger and then did a little French. After 1st dinner we wheeled by the Grand Column and beyond Wimille and were caught by the rain. Came home through the valley.

SUNDAY, AUGUST 20

Today is the great day in Boulogne and environs. The great procession left the cathedral about 3 p.m. and proceeded down town through Porte de Dune and Grand Rue. Stevie and Tate were to see it. Clare worked all day and I was off in the morning.

MONDAY, AUGUST 21

No entry

TUESDAY, AUGUST 22

No entry

WEDNESDAY, AUGUST 23

Had my half day and Fred and I wheeled to Souvin Moulin for dinner. Came home by Wimille.

THURSDAY, AUGUST 24

Stevie had her p.m. I had morning hours. Clare and McConnell go for leave tomorrow I believe.

FRIDAY, AUGUST 25

Clare and McConnell really did get off this a.m. with their leave dated from yesterday I believe. I did not see Clare this morning.

SATURDAY, AUGUST 26

No entry

SUNDAY, AUGUST 27

Sunderland came over from Convalescent Camp, and he and I went for a walk after dinner. He is an exceptionally nice boy and very interesting to me. So many things in common. I hate to see him go up the line again.

MONDAY, AUGUST 28

Walked back to Souvin Moulin with S. this afternoon. Such a nice walk and dinner. Miss Eastwood and Capt. T. were there too. We came home by Wimille, getting home about 10. Sunderland is a marvel avoiding complications as to rules.

TUESDAY, AUGUST 29

Two box[es] of chocolates from Ray and a book I had asked for. Sunderland was to see us this a.m. to say goodbye as he is off to Étaples today. We will miss him very much.

WEDNESDAY, AUGUST 30

A card from Laurie Snowball today.

THURSDAY, AUGUST 31

Two cards form Clare, one written in London and the other from Leicester. She and Cyril are having pleasant jaunts together. I miss Clare terribly these days especially. Am glad though that she is having a nice holiday.

Ruth confides many and various observations in her diary, including her impression of a church service on September 3 as simply "horrid." In anticipation of Clare's return, Ruth fixes up her hut with both curtains and flowers, a gesture greatly appreciated by Clare who terms it "beautifully arranged."[62] *Despite the busyness in the hospital, or perhaps due to it, Ruth and Clare find time to go bike riding and, at month's end, "tramping" about a local forest with a young French boy harvesting mushrooms. Ruth even has another visit from her Australian admirer, Edward Sunderland, who appears on leave from nearby Étaples on the twenty-fourth. Some things, however, grow even worse. The Battle of the Somme wears on but now with a difference. By mid-September it is Canadian soldiers who are pouring into No. 3 CGH nightly by the hundreds. The Canadian Corps has been moved to the Somme and are now fighting at Courcelette. This influx of Canadian wounded is reflected in Ruth's diary by the daily recording of the number of wounded in each convoy from the fifteenth of the month onwards. Ruth often speaks of receiving or not receiving patients, which usually refers to the specific ward on which she is working that day. She also records the death of men she knew, including Roy Gaynor of Chatham, and of others known to her fellow nurses, like Captain Lehancer. She also takes note of news about family members who are serving, gleaned from wounded men passing through No. 3 CGH. Two instances of this are Harold Desbrisay, a former medical student from Ruth's Montreal days, and Fred Buck,[63] a fellow New Brunswicker. Ruth writes to Buck's mother with news of her son's condition.*

FRIDAY, SEPTEMBER 1

I wrote Clare and redirected her letters. New sisters, six of them, are to arrive tomorrow. We are wondering who they are.

SATURDAY, SEPTEMBER 2

Stevie and I went wheeling after dinner, down the Calais road to Wimille and then out to Wimereux and home by the Convalescent Camp. The new sisters have just arrived. 3 RVH and 2 Western and one NY graduate. Miss Long and Dora Jones are in London.

SUNDAY, SEPTEMBER 3

A windy day. Off last hours and feel lost. Went to a horrid service at 5:45. A nice solo by the Australian who sang for us before, and Dr. Davis gave us a treat with his accompanying. There was a fine singsong in the Y.M.[64] this evening, Dr. Davis conducting.

MONDAY, SEPTEMBER 4

Miss Doherty Western is in S with us. I took early hours. We received medical cases last night and are quite full up. We went tonight to a Concert Militaire given in Boulogne, offered (as the program said) to the Allied Troops of the Boulogne garrison. A wonderful pianist from the Conserval Paris treated us to Chopin and Lizst, and a good orchestra played the Meditation from Faust beautifully. There was ballet dancing, and everything was conducted French fashion even to mixing up our tickets. It was very late when we got home—after midnight—but the concert was worth it.

TUESDAY, SEPTEMBER 5

A blowy rainy day. We are filled up with medicals again. Miss Clark is resigning and I go on night duty when she leaves. Miss Doughty goes to "R" tomorrow. Stevie relieved in F this p.m. Had a card from Laura today and a letter from Isabel MacNaughton. Who has regained strength slowly. Donald has enlisted, in what I do not know. No letters from home yet.

WEDNESDAY, SEPTEMBER 6

A busy morning. I had my half day. I put up Clare's curtains and fixed her flowers. After tea Nettie Tate and I went down town. I got some fruit for Benger and some glasses and spoons for the ward. In the evening Nettie and I went back to the garden for flowers, dahlias and roses.

Had a letter from Helen and Irene L. and one from MacKenzie and a couple from patients. It has been a beautiful day. The hospital is full of medical cases, which makes me think of winter. Clare comes tomorrow night I think. Am sorry she will find a roommate waiting for her.

THURSDAY, SEPTEMBER 7

Bert Gourlay and I went down to meet Clare and McConnell, and the Matron of the District brought us home in an ambulance. We had supper in Stevie's room. It is great to have Clare back. She sleeps in Edith's room tonight.

FRIDAY, SEPTEMBER 8

Clare brought a nice sweater for Mama and me a picture and a Cheshire cat knocker. Clare in W today.

SATURDAY, SEPTEMBER 9

Last hours and Clare and I went down to the old town for tea and shopping. There was a tennis match on this p.m. between No. 1 officers and ours, and our men won. The hospital is very quiet, mostly medical cases. I fixed up the sweater for mailing and sent Ray the song.

SUNDAY, SEPTEMBER 10

Benger had a party in S today. He is in khaki again and on duty. Nott and I fed the bunnies after seven. There are 2 new little pigs. Two boxes of sweets from Ray and a letter from Len and one from Edward Sunderland.

MONDAY, SEPTEMBER 11

No entry

TUESDAY, SEPTEMBER 12

Stevie and Tate and Lill and I went down to Boulogne for dinner. A letter from Ray today.

Miss McConnell and I started for a ride tonight, but my pedal dropped off at Wimille so we walked home through the valley. My wheel is certainly unfortunate. Letters from Len and Murray tonight.

WEDNESDAY, SEPTEMBER 13

Clare and I had our p.m.s and went bicycling (I on Connie's) straight out the St. Omer road, through Boulogne Forest, turning aside to our left to visit Le Wast and then on to Colembert where we had tea in a most extraordinary room and extraordinary tea made in a jug, and Clare swears the old man's tobacco got mixed up with the tea. Jambon, mashed up, was so uninviting that we had our usual omelet, our old standby. We came home by Wierre-Effroy and up the big hill and home by St. Martins. It was a lovely ride and we were in time for dinner.

THURSDAY, SEPTEMBER 14

On duty tonight. The ward is light and we are not receiving. Orders to evacuate though today.

It is a beautiful cold, clear night. Miss Clark[65] leaves tomorrow for England. She and I had supper with Naomi Gray in Ward O. Mushrooms and chops. Pte. Buck from the 55th, in H with a bullet through his lung and doing well. Miss Burt saw his letter addressed to Len and told me of it.

FRIDAY, SEPTEMBER 15

Convoy: 329

It is dark and stormy looking tonight. Miss Clark got off today after lunch. It is noisy, sleeping as the workmen are close by building huts for CC or BD. A couple of letters from patients' families today. Three new sisters came to us today—2 Jeffry Hall nurses and the other American trained, all strangers. Janet Rodd came to S this a.m. Naomi tells that our old friend Mead has been killed. She had a letter from his mother. Convoys last night. 300 received.

SATURDAY, SEPTEMBER 16

Another beautiful night. I went down town this a.m. with Mrs. Giffron and Miss Bert MacDougal. Had my hair washed and got "Les Miserables," which I had ordered long ago at Mendues. The "boy" was in attendance as usual. Got some fruit for young Buck who has been transferred to the Red Cross tent. A big evacuation today and two convoys expected tonight. I begin night with eight patients. Roy Gaynor[66] is killed.

SUNDAY, SEPTEMBER 17

A letter from Ray tonight. Nice and newsy. Dickie is on in "B" and Watling Night Supervisor. Clare goes on in O. A stormy night and receiving all night. Wrote Ray and Len and Murray. We evacuated twenty-five today. Desbrisay[67] from Chatham here. Says Roy Gaynor is killed. Convoy: 263

MONDAY, SEPTEMBER 18

A large evacuation today. Desbrisay went to England. He told me that Walter and Warrie were quite alright as far as he knew. Fred Buck will go to England shortly. I wrote Mrs. Buck tonight. 452 received.

TUESDAY, SEPTEMBER 19

Mrs. Giffin and I went down to No. 7, Mrs. G. to see a 25th officer who gave her information about a friend of theirs, Capt. Lehancer, who is thought to have been killed. I got some fruit for Buck and sent him Len's letter to read. (Came this a.m.) Ninety-one in convoy.

WEDNESDAY, SEPTEMBER 20

Fred Buck went to England this a.m. I gave him my last 1£ note. He will pay it back to Len. There are terrible cases in the Red Cross hut. I am glad to be in S even though we must send the majority to Convalescent Camp. I finished reading *Anna Karenina* tonight.

136 in tonight's convoy.

THURSDAY, SEPTEMBER 21

I slept from 9 a.m. till 6:10 tonight and felt the better for it. No mail today. Two convoys tonight but my share is very small. We evacuated tonight.

Camiers, Aug.–Nov.15: 3,041
Boulogne, Feb.–July 21: 14,325
Admit July 1st to July 21: 6,006
Deaths during July: 42

FRIDAY, SEPTEMBER 22

Lill, Clare, and I went down town. I took my bicycle to be mended, and we bought oilcloth for our room. We will have a man put it down and paper our walls. How we dread the winter. It has been a beautiful day and is bright and cold tonight. I did not sleep well, as a result of getting to bed late. The search lights were busy tonight, and hundreds of rockets appeared to the north. Our lights went off but were on again in a short time. There was gun firing in the southeast, a long distance away but we could see the flashes. The convoys are from the Somme tonight. I got twenty-five, mostly Canadians. Convoys: 112.

SATURDAY, SEPTEMBER 23

A quiet night. Not receiving. Sunderland is down on pass from Étaples to see us. Such a surprise. Small convoy, fifty-nine.

SUNDAY, SEPTEMBER 24

Convoy: 175

MONDAY, SEPTEMBER 25

A year ago since Loos. Small convoy, fifty-six.

TUESDAY, SEPTEMBER 26

Have just received thirty-nine mixed surgical and medical. A letter from Len tonight says he is in a draft to the 26th at last and will be in France any day. Am glad for his sake he is getting over. He enclosed a letter from Fred Buck who is in the Edmonton Military Hospital, London. No news from Walter yet. The water was off all night, which made receiving difficult. Total convoy: 244.

WEDNESDAY, SEPTEMBER 27

Lill off duty with fomentation to her eye. Bert Gourlay is taking her place for the night. Have a nice letter from Ray tonight and a paper. Clare and I got up for a French lesson at 5:30 thinking today was Thursday. There were convoys today: 127 and one tonight, so 136. News from the Somme is particularly good. Combles is really ours and the French have taken Frignicourt and Rancourt.

THURSDAY, SEPTEMBER 28

Lill still off duty but her eye is much better. Clare and I went tramping this a.m. looking for mushrooms. A nice fourteen-year-old French boy joined us and showed us the best pastures.

He is to meet us in the morning and take us farther afield. Our little friend goes to school in Paris and is a very serious minded young man. A convoy came in today and there has been a large one tonight: 207 with a number of bad cases. We are not receiving. A letter came from Walter tonight. He is ok as yet. The lights are off tonight again.

FRIDAY, SEPTEMBER 29

A letter from Fred Buck tonight. Clare and I went mushroom hunting with our friend of yesterday. We had a fine tramp over many a field and got two good baskets full. Roy Genister was singing in our ante hut when we got home, which made going to bed still later. Slept well today. It is dark and windy tonight with rain at intervals. Mr. Lloyd George speaks his mind to Neutrals in today's paper and warns them to keep hands off. Mr. Gerard[68] has left Berlin for U.S. 120 patients in.

SATURDAY, SEPTEMBER 30

A grand day for sleeping, though Clare had a wakeful night of it. There is a heavy dew tonight and occasional showers. Had a letter from Caddick and wrote him and Mrs. Grey and Walter. Have been reading such a nice article in the Geographic magazine on France. Convoys again tonight but we are not receiving. The time changes tonight so we have thirteen and one-half hours' duty. 182 received last night.

October begins with the convoys of wounded still arriving. Ruth is so busy that on ten of the days of the month, she makes no entries except for convoy numbers on five of those days. On twelve of the first fifteen days of October, she records the number of wounded arriving at No. 3 CGH. Then the rains begin. The one blessing of miserable weather is that it slows the rate of warfare and as a consequence the flow of wounded. Sometimes the entire

No. 3 CGH (with a capacity of over two thousand beds) is full and the wounded have to be redirected to one of the other hospitals nearby.

In the midst of the misery Ruth has three bright spots. First, there are letters. Some come from former patients recovering in England, others are newsy letters from home, especially from her sister Ray. Second, late in the month, her admirer Sunderland visits again. It is at this time that Ruth's friend Clare confides to her diary that "Sunderland, the Australian, appeared again at Ward S today on pass from his Étaples base...[he] is a big, fine looking physical specimen, with an atmosphere of 'winds in the open' about him."[69] Finally, there is the distraction and release of little celebrations. The nurses have a quiet meal in their mess, but Ruth and her fellow ward nurse Stevie work and decorate in order to have a Halloween party for the "up patients" in their ward. It is a success. As a favour, Clare even writes out invitations in rhyme for all Ruth's patients. Ruth saves a copy in her diary, which appears below.

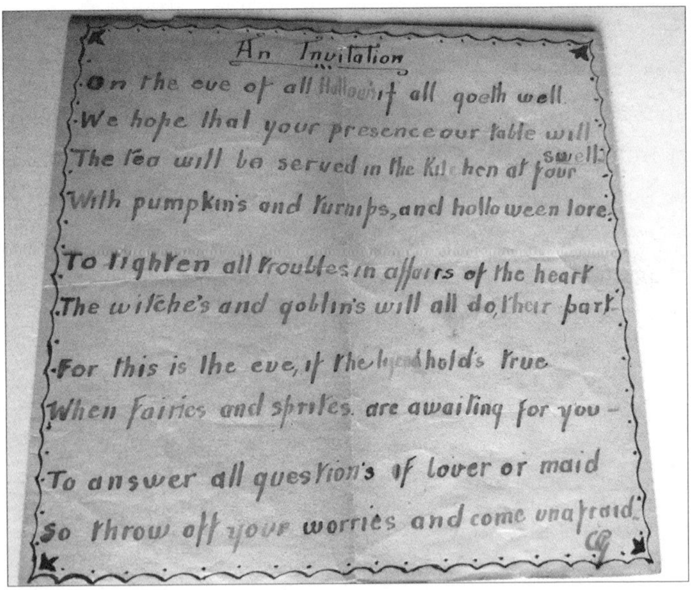

An Invitation

On the eve of all Hallowe'en if all goeth well
We hope that your presence our table will swell
The tea will be served in the Kitchen at four
With pumpkin's and turnips, and hollo ween lore.

To lighten all troubles in affairs of the heart
The witche's and goblin's will all do their part

For this is the eve, if the legend holds true
When fairies and sprites are awaiting for you –

To answer all question's of lover or maid
So throw off your worries and come unafraid.
CG

Clare's hand-written Halloween invitation.

SUNDAY, OCTOBER 1

No entry

MONDAY, OCTOBER 2

Convoy: 189

TUESDAY, OCTOBER 3

Convoy: 65

WEDNESDAY, OCTOBER 4

Convoy: 162

THURSDAY, OCTOBER 5

No entry

FRIDAY, OCTOBER 6

282 in convoy

Reta Powell's resignation is in. She wants to go to her sister who has been seriously ill. No news of Mann's resignation yet.[70]

SATURDAY, OCTOBER 7

Small convoy of eighty-one.

SUNDAY, OCTOBER 8

Clare got up for church. I slept right through. Three convoys in tonight and we have all beds full. Just sixty in last night.

MONDAY, OCTOBER 9

Wrote home tonight. A box of apples arrived last evening from Aunt Mamie. They were not in very good condition. My veils came from Blooms[71] today. 114 in convoy tonight.

TUESDAY, OCTOBER 10

Another very windy night and the service tent is very shaky. Three convoys are coming in—S receiving third on the list. We got up for Mr. Makins' concert this afternoon. It was very good and the patients enjoyed it immensely. Lill had a letter from home today. Her mother is well but Mr. Smith has had a bad heart attack. No word of Lill or Mann's orders coming through. I slept very badly today. 110 patients in.

WEDNESDAY, OCTOBER 11

Convoy of 137

Stevie and I went to No. 14 Stationary this p.m. to see Withers and Card. Clare came too to see Anderson. We each took some reading material along. A letter from Ray tonight. Such a nice one. They have been camping and were going to P.E.I. for a trip, the girls and Wilbur. Mama is quite herself again. Mrs. Murray and little Miss Morrison were visiting. Irene Greaves has a son. It will be the wonderful child. Watling's home letter said that Muriel Baldwin and Ethel McEwen were married. I forget to whom. Mrs. Watling is much better and Em thinks of returning to work. Lill had a letter from Murray saying Wm. Smith is better.

THURSDAY, OCTOBER 12

Convoy seventy-five

A letter from Mr. Archibald tonight. He is enjoying a leave before starting his studies. I will send him Murray's address.

Mr. A. is going to Scotland for a few days. Another windy rainy night. We are not receiving.

FRIDAY, OCTOBER 13

Four convoys in, 204 total last night.

Lill and I cleaned our room, which has been very untidy since papering. We are going to be very comfortable. I slept all day till six. Another blowy day with a drizzly rain for company. Wrote Mr. Archibald and Len enclosing Ray's. Also wrote Westaway and Alice Kitchen. We have twenty C's & D's on the evacuation list but are only sending B cases in the a.m.[72]

SATURDAY, OCTOBER 14

Convoy of twenty patients last night. A cold windy night. Miss Nichols was here to dinner on her way to Le Tréport. She gave us all the news about Col G. etc. A couple of letters from patients. Clare and I went down to Boulogne and had our hair washed, and I ordered a dressing gown for Ray's birthday. Also bought a chain for my Joan d'Arc pendant.

SUNDAY, OCTOBER 15

A letter from Murray this evening. He is in the C Records office. Wrote him of Mr. A's whereabouts and wrote home. Such an effort. There is to be receiving tonight.

MONDAY, OCTOBER 16

A very cold night and no fires in the wards yet. It seems very unnecessary suffering.

TUESDAY, OCTOBER 17

Such a miserable night last night. Cold and I was so sick. I did not sleep at all today in consequence. No letters today.

WEDNESDAY, OCTOBER 18

Quite an exciting night last night. An irrational pneumonia patient who got up on occasion when left alone and, in the early a.m., a shell shock case disappeared and was located in No. 1. He (Ellis) became quite violent when brought home, and before 6 a.m. we had the M.O. and four orderlies and a patient on hand to keep Ellis in bed. Had letter from Gustefson who has been operated on in England and one from Herior. I slept all day and feel the better for it. No letter from Len yet.

THURSDAY, OCTOBER 19

A rainy night last night. Ellis was irrational all night and had to be watched. The pneumonia case was transferred to Z today.

FRIDAY, OCTOBER 20

Ellis was evacuated to England today.

SATURDAY, OCTOBER 21

Sunderland appeared on the scene this evening on pass, which he will take good care to overstay. Another cold night but bright and clear. My pneumonia case died in Z today.

SUNDAY, OCTOBER 22

S and I went down to the ramparts for an hour, then had tea before coming home. The Sunday morning strollers on the ramparts were very droll. I went to the office and asked for our [Clare and Ruth's] passes for tomorrow, and they are delivered to me here tonight.

MONDAY, OCTOBER 23

Off night duty and Clare and I went to Calais by train. Instead of leaving the station at 10, the train did not come until after 12. I dozed most of the train journey. Calais is quite a modern looking town and quite as clean as Boulogne. We visited the Church of Notre Dame and walked past the house where Lady Hamilton died. Then on through the fishing folk.

TUESDAY, OCTOBER 24

The morning after the night before. Slept in till noon and went on duty with a head like a drum. I am taking a cold sure enough.

WEDNESDAY, OCTOBER 25–SUNDAY, OCTOBER 29

No entries

MONDAY, OCTOBER 30

Stevie has been in hollowing pumpkins and turnips for our party tomorrow night. It has been another rainy day with heavy showers and a high wind.

TUESDAY, OCTOBER 31

Our party came off tonight and was a real success. Stevie and I shopped in the morning in the rain. All the guests came and we had chicken and ham, scalloped potatoes and rolls, and fruit and cream. Then there were rolls and fruit and nuts all round for the patients. McRae and Taylor and Booth and Nott and Steele and L'Heureux and our staff filled the table in the kitchen, and Metcalfe entertained the crowd. A letter from Murray tonight.

The bad weather continues, even intensifies, with the new month. However, it brings with it the collateral effect of fewer convoys. On the downside, Ruth and her fellow nurses also experience the effects of the rains and the cold. Both Ruth and Clare suffer recurring headaches throughout the month, perhaps a function of both the cold and the fumes from the small hut stoves. Their hut also leaks and a steady fuel supply is not secured for the stoves until the seventeenth. Ruth and Clare, along with other nurses, continue their little outings in spite of the persistent rain. There is a costume dance in the Red Cross hut on the fourth, and Ruth even has to contend with a letter from an English admirer, named Clark. Clare reveals that he sent Ruth a not too subtly titled gift book, "Romance of the Oxford Colleges."[73] Ruth struggles with how to write him a letter, which he will surely regret receiving, but she expresses relief once having done so.

Other letters, a persistent outlet and source of coping, continue to flow. There are letters from former patients recovering in England, from new Canadian soldiers arriving at camps in England, letters from friends in Montreal (see November 17), and of course, correspondence from friends and family back in New Brunswick. The diary's repeated references to the arrival or non-arrival of mail and Ruth's animated and engaged interaction with all this correspondence speaks volumes as to its importance. Surrounded as she is by misfortune and pain, this correspondence serves an anchoring function, a counter to her own griefs and worries, a touchstone with home and normal life. In the midst of the storm that is the Great War, it grounds her, reminding her of what and where she comes from, of who she is, and that she, unlike so many, still has a future to consider and anticipate. Like her diary to which she commits both her activities and her thoughts, this correspondence is a lifeline in the midst of the chaos and turbulence of the Great War.

WEDNESDAY, NOVEMBER 1

Miss Bert had her p.m. today and I had morning hours. Spent in putting up shelves. It will be so nice to get fixed up again. Letters from Len and one of our patients at No. 14 Stationary. Len has been in the trenches and likes the chaps in the 26th very much. Clark[74] went to B.D.[75] today, also Sunbeam who has been his shadow these past few days.

THURSDAY, NOVEMBER 2

Had morning hours and Stevie had her half day. The French men are putting in our stoves at last, and it is time as we are all very dirty. Had a letter from Fred Buck tonight. He expects to be in bed for two months yet. There was a large convoy last night. This has been a blowy rainy day.

FRIDAY, NOVEMBER 3

Clare's and my half day. We had our hair washed and went to see Mollie who is better and going to England for three weeks' sick leave. We got back into Boulogne in the D.D.W.'s[76] car and did some shopping on the way home. I left some parcels at No. 14 for our ex-patients. The afternoon began fine but turned rainy before we got home. Another large convoy last night.

SATURDAY, NOVEMBER 4

A fine day for a change but a rainy evening for the dance. I had morning hours and wrote letters. Len and a couple of patients, and I redirected Lill's letters home. Had a letter from her today. She and Mann expected to sail today on transports. I went and looked on for a few minutes at the dance. Splendid costumes and the Red Cross hut has a good floor. Miss Burt was in Kilts and Stevie represents France, Edith and Edith S. were both well gotten up—

all the costumes were good. Savage brought a book to me tonight from Clark, and I feel very much at a loss to know how to write him. I will enjoy the book, which is on Oxford College nevertheless.

MONDAY, NOVEMBER 6

I had an hour before lunch and then relieved in the pneumonia hut. And got off duty at 6 p.m. No mail today. Clare isn't feeling well. Has a bad headache.

TUESDAY, NOVEMBER 7

Had last hours from 3:30. Clare went to bed and I brought dinner to her. Lou Gillis called on us, also Naomi Gray and Watling who is on special leave tomorrow. No mail today.

WEDNESDAY, NOVEMBER 8

Clare and L slept in and had the whole day off. Breakfast in our room in luxurious fashion about 9:30, and after lunch we went to the cemetery to locate Reilly's grave and then down town. We went to a Meridew's and were waited on by our friend. I got a frame for Dean and we bought several little necessities. A mail tonight but nothing for me, except a letter from Conibear who is going to England. After dinner I painted our extra table white and it will look nice with a green top. Babbit and Handcock and Miss Robinson are back from leave, and Watling and McGreer and Walters and McGiffin crossed this a.m. Lill and Mann were to sail on Sunday from Liverpool. Lill bought mufti, which did not arrive in time.

THURSDAY, NOVEMBER 9

Have just written Clark, which is a load off my mind. Also wrote Mrs. Skeates and Miss Conibear and Pte. Cord. Quite an evening's work. Clare is at a concert, but I feel my evening to be very profitable. No mail for me again today. Babbit brought Dickie's suit to me and I'll send it on Sunday. Had morning hours and cleaned the room. We received some locals today, and I heard the fall in a short while ago. The port is closed again this p.m. we hear. More channel troubles.

FRIDAY, NOVEMBER 10

Stevie slept in and went to Camiers for the day. The Matron and Edith Stevenson went with her in the car.

SATURDAY, NOVEMBER 11

Miss Bert's day off and we had a rather busy day.

SUNDAY, NOVEMBER 12

Wrote home and got a letter from home tonight, one from Mrs. Grey and two and a card from L.

MONDAY, NOVEMBER 13

A nice mild day for our trip. The ride out of here was very nice. Things have changed around Camiers. German prisoners in hundreds were building new railroads, and the training camp near Étaples has extended up over the dunes back of the road and right up to the cemetery. We caught the car to Paris Plage and had a nice time there at the Swiss Shop. Back to Étaples on the 4 p.m. train, and then we walked to No. 1 and saw Dixon and Miss Young. Of course, I had a headache and had a miserable late afternoon. The train was an hour late only and we got home in good time. I bought some val lace for Helen Donald and some insertion and edging for myself.

TUESDAY, NOVEMBER 14

Had first hours after lunch and went down town to send magazines to my boys. Also got some Xmas cards. A nice mail for me tonight. Nott and Steele and a yard long one from Conibear who is in Oxford. A card from Morgan and a letter from Aggie Richardson. Madge Fraser is with Mrs. Cape's baby who has had pneumonia. Mrs. Carlisle is better and things at No. 23 are in their usual unsatisfactory state. Had note from Miss Coulter who is ill at Chateau Meurieaun.

WEDNESDAY, NOVEMBER 15

Had last hours and went down to see Miss Coulter. She looks very tired and ill but is feeling better now. She found the work at C very hard but liked it. I wheeled down alone and called at 14 Stationary Hospital to see Cpl. MacRae. Both he and Jock are marked up for Blighty. A letter from Tini Watling tonight written at the Thacory. They had a very pleasant time with their brothers Wallie and Max and Louise McGreer's two brothers, and Murray was in to tea. Tini says looks splendid. Warrie L. is wounded and in England.[77] The 132nd are over.[78] Tini saw the Mersereau's in the bank. A Canadian mail tonight but none for me.

THURSDAY, NOVEMBER 16

No entry

FRIDAY, NOVEMBER 17

Came off duty to find a real fire in our room. The varnish smell but oh what a comfort to have the warmth. A letter from Miss Watson today. She is confined to the house as usual. Mr. Watson is well for him, and Miss Langford is at work in the R.V. Paul is war crazy Miss W. says but will not be allowed to leave till next year. She is wise.

SATURDAY, NOVEMBER 18

Clare and I went down town early afternoon hours. We got flowers and I brought my frame home and bought a silver box for Lill and a collar for Bernice and a couple of "Canada" to send to Len and Walter. A rainy day as usual and the fire, when once on, is good. Got Mother's dressing gown and Ray's and Helen's things ready for mailing.

SUNDAY, NOVEMBER 19

A rainy day again and our room is leaking badly.[79] I spent most of my time off cleaning up, making a fire and fixing the roof. We got last night's mail today but none for me. Wrote home and to Len and Smith. Naomi and Stevie came in for reading last evening.

MONDAY, NOVEMBER 20

No mail for me today. I had early hours and went down to the bank and got my picture "Love and Life" a new glass. It looks very lovely now. Spent the remainder of the time off cleaning the room. Our ashes are taken away for us today, so that is an improvement. Another windy, rainy day and our roof still leaks.

TUESDAY, NOVEMBER 21

Such a nice day for a change. Our roof fixed this afternoon. Clare's and my afternoon. We planned a bicycle ride, but mine has a puncture so we walked to Souverain-Moulin instead.
Had tea and pancakes and came home by the road. Miss Eastwood frequents. We walked to S through the valley and Wimille. The girls are due back tonight, but MacH has a telegram from C.M.W.[80] to say that the train missed the boat. A mail tonight and I have a letter from Cliff Loggie. Wonders never cease. I am to go to Ward G in the morning. Have a bad eye tonight and a headache in consequence.

WEDNESDAY, NOVEMBER 22

The girls got back at lunch time and report a splendid holiday. McGiffin and Murray had a nice time together, and the girls all liked Murray very much. Watling has letters from home saying that Mrs. Dickie is failing. I hope Lill gets there in time to be of use. I had a letter from Watts tonight. Stevie and Clare and I went to Australian hospital[81] tonight for dinner and had a lovely time. Their hut hospital will be very nice when completed. The girls are a bright, wide awake bunch, and we enjoyed their pictures and accounts of life in Egypt very much. We had a busy day in G—two deaths. I am to go back to S in the morning.

THURSDAY, NOVEMBER 23

Morning hours. We hear from Capt. Henderson that S2 will be turned into a Convalescent Ward for PUO's.[82] Stevie goes on night duty tonight.[83]

NOTES

1 These three McGill nurses were on leave in London and came to see their compatriots at Cliveden and convey the latest relocation news from France.

2 This appears to be nurse shorthand for debilitated, or simply worn down, men.

3 Clare Gass's diary (Jan. 14, 1916) informs us that this was Ruth's cousin Grace who was in England at the time.

4 Approximately six miles (10 km) to Stokes Poges and another seven miles (12 km) to Windsor Castle.

5 Nine pence in the British pre-decimal coinage system.

6 Perhaps the forty-four-year-old Corey Clark of Newcastle mentioned in the 1911 census.

7 Edith Leslie, born Montreal 1878, graduated RVH 1912, enlisted in CAMC April 22, 1915.

8 Ruth means a letter that came direct to her new English address instead of being redirected from France.

9 This entry marks the end of the 1915 volume of Ruth's diary. She had written in the unused January portion of her 1915 edition. February's entries commence the 1916 journal volume.

10 See Mann, War Diary of Clare Gass, which contains several photographs.

11 Christina and Helen Arnoldi, biological sisters, born in Ottawa and belonging to the "Laval Unit" and obviously well known to Ruth through Montreal nursing connections.
12 Queen Alexandra's Imperial Military Nursing Service (QAIMNS) Reserve was a British Great War nursing service.
13 The Feb. 6, 1916, war diary entry for the Duchess of Connaught Canadian Red Cross Hospital, Taplow, shows that "A Court of Enquiry...will assemble for the purpose of investigating and reporting on the work and conduct of Sister S. Burns." No further details are recorded.
14 An unrecorded incident in ward "Alex 1" is noted but not expounded upon in Clare Gass's diary as well.
15 Ruth's cousins Murray Anderson (111007) and Walter Anderson (111601), members of the 6 CMR who enlisted in May 1915.
16 Charlotte L. MacNaughton, born Sherbrooke, NS, graduated MGH 1904, joined CAMC April 22, 1915. She was suffering from appendicitis.
17 CGD, March 20, 1916.
18 Barbara Lamont, born Elmwood, ON, 1870, enlisted in London, England, Oct. 4, 1915.
19 Clearly Ruth's first anniversary of service weighs on her mind. Technically, they heard of the move on March 4 and actually went to Quebec by train on March 6 (CGD, March 4–7).
20 Beatrice Louise Armitage, born Cleveland, PQ, 1885, graduated MGH 1913, enlisted CAMC April 22, 1915.
21 See note 76 in the 1915 entries.
22 An old expression similar to saying "I feel like two cents," meaning tired and useless.
23 Ruth's thoughts trail off at this point, and she leaves her diary entry exactly like this.
24 Violet E. Sampson, born Quebec 1878, graduated MGH 1907, enlisted in CAMC April 15, 1915.
25 Julia Marjorie Ross, born Montreal 1888, graduated MGH 1914, enlisted in CAMC April 22, 1915.
26 CGD, April 26, 1915.
27 Convalescent Camp.
28 One of a series of books by English novelist and playwright John Glasworthy.
29 Nurses from Queen's University who had served in the Mediterranean as part of No. 5 Canadian Stationary Hospital were now moved to France and the entire unit renamed No. 7 Canadian General Hospital.
30 Mabel Keith Douglas, born at Belfast, Ireland, 1882, joined CAMC at Kingston, ON, May 5, 1915, acting matron of No. 5 CSH serving in England briefly and then in Cairo, Egypt, before a temporary posting at No. 3 CGH.
31 Wilfred L. Churchill (90281), born at Short Beach, Yarmouth Co., NS, admitted to No. 3 CGH April 16 with facial burns. Would return to duty to suffer gunshot wounds, influenza, pneumonia, and measles while serving and being awarded the Military Cross (20-10-1916) and gold bar (26-4-1917: Vimy Ridge).
32 Sophia Mary Hoerner, born Montreal 1877, graduated MGH 1898, enlisted in CAMC April 22, 1915.

33 Winifred Brown, born Montreal 1884, enlisted in CAMC at Montreal, the Laval Unit, Jan. 31, 1916.
34 Aimee Isobel Maud Hobkirk, born England 1888, enlisted in CAMC, the Laval Unit, at Montreal, Dec. 29, 1915.
35 Frances MacKeen, born Glace Bay, NS, 1889, graduated RVH 1913, enlisted in CAMC April 22, 1915.
36 Voluntary Aid Detachment. Slightly trained assistants to the nurses, but definitely not trained nurses. The CAMC's matron-in-chief was very hesitant to employ them, partly out of fear they would undermine the professional image of nursing.
37 Home sisters were not nurses but were essentially domestic staff whose task was to do housekeeping work for the nursing sisters so that they could focus on professional nursing with limited distractions.
38 Provost Army Office, in charge of policing travel and movement within the war zone.
39 Army Provost Marshall.
40 United Free Church of Scotland, one of the many subdivisions of Presbyterianism found in Scotland at the time.
41 That segment of a Presbyterian worship service conducted by the head clergyman.
42 Capt. James MacNaughton, born Black River, NB, 1881, enlisted Aug. 31, 1915, in the 55th Infantry Battalion.
43 Capt. Herbert Little, born London, ON, 1887, enlisted CAMC March 5, 1915, one of the doctors of the McGill Unit who had the unit's automobile that day.
44 Muriel Clark, born Hamilton, ON, 1877, graduated MGH 1908, enlisted in CAMC April 22, 1915.
45 Dennis G. Gould (70206), born Chatham, NB, 1884, enlisted in 26th Infantry Battalion April 1915.
46 Netley was a large British Army Hospital located outside Southampton in England.
47 CGD, July 9, 1916.
48 Margaret Jane Fortescue, born York Factory, Man., 1878, graduated MGH 1906, enlisted in CAMC April 22, 1915.
49 Ruth means "walking" or "crawling" with lice since the uniforms are now being left on the men instead of taken off immediately.
50 Deputy Director Medical Services.
51 Katherine A. MacLeod, born Glasgow, Scotland, 1892, graduated MGH 1914, enlisted in CAMC April 22, 1915.
52 German planes successfully bombed an ammunition depot in the Calais area.
53 Admissions and Discharges.
54 CGD, August 26–Sept. 3, 1916.
55 Edward H. Sunderland of New South Wales, who enlisted in the Australian Expeditionary Force August 29, 1914. He was admitted to No. 3 CGH August 10, 1916, and later convalesced in nearby institutions. In September 1918 he married an English woman before returning to Australia (National Archives of Australia file).

56 Private Albert Baxendale (320), born Leyland, England, 1886, listed his profession as X-ray assistant on his attestation form when he enlisted at Montreal on March 18, 1915.

57 Likely Constance M. Stuart, born Rochester, England, 1889, graduated MGH 1912, enlisted in CAMC April 20, 1915.

58 Kaireen MacKay, born Eau Claire, ON, 1888, graduated RVH 1914, enlisted in CAMC April 22, 1915.

59 Janet M. Rodd, born Charlottletown, PEI, 1886, graduated RVH 1913, enlisted in CAMC April 14, 1915.

60 Doctors and orderlies belonging to the Queen's University Unit can now move to their new location at No. 7 CGH.

61 Title supplied by Clare Gass diary, August 17, 1916. Ruth had left a blank space.

62 CGD, Sept. 7, 1916.

63 Fred Buck (444318) of Woodstock, NB, enlisted in 24th Battery CFA, Dec. 30, 1914, wounded Sept. 9, 1916, and admitted to No. 3 CGH Sept. 14 before being sent on to hospital in England.

64 An abbreviation for YMCA (Young Men's Christian Association).

65 Nursing Sister Clark's mother was very ill, and Miss Clark was allowed to return to Canada (CGD, Sept. 15).

66 Roy F. Gaynor (111188), born Chatham, NB, 1893, joined 5 CMR April 10, 1915, killed in action Sept. 14, 1915.

67 Most likely Harold A. Desbrisay (1969), who enlisted in the CAMC on Nov. 30, 1914, recording his calling as a "medical student." By July 1917 he was a surgeon and an officer.

68 James W. Gerard, the American ambassador to Germany 1913–1917. He finally left Germany later in 1917 after having been detained by the Germans who had heard rumours that the German ambassador in America was being mistreated and that German ships were being detained and their contents confiscated. Both rumours proved untrue.

69 CGD, Oct. 21, 1916.

70 Perhaps Jane F. Mann (see note 86 in the 1915 entries).

71 A famous London department store of the period.

72 Apparently a reference to an in-house triage system whereby patients were rated as to the severity of their wounds and their ability to be moved to other nearby institutions or by boat to England.

73 CGD, Nov. 4, 1916.

74 Most likely the Clark mentioned by Clare as Ruth's other admirer. He had "a narrow, clean cut face with regular features and is the product of one of the great old universities of England" (CGD, Oct. 21, 1916).

75 Base Depot, a necessary step on the way back to the trenches.

76 Deputy Director Wimereaux. In her diary, Clare Gass states that it was a Red Cross car (Mann, 148).

77 Warren Loggie (110329), born Chatham, NB, 1889, joined the 5 CMR in April 1915 and suffered a gunshot wound in the right thigh in early October 1915 on the Somme. He was later promoted to lieutenant, received the Distinguished Conduct Medal and the Military Cross for bravery.

78 The 132nd Infantry Battalion based in Newcastle, NB, was raised from men in Ruth's part of New Brunswick.

79 Apparently the army's purpose-built huts meant to accommodate two nurses' sleeping quarters and a small common area were not really up to the weather conditions of northern France.
80 Christina Mary Watling.
81 Australian No. 2 General Hospital (CGD, Nov. 22, 1916).
82 Pyrexia of unknown origin, a vague medical term to describe fever and pains. It was similar to Trench Fever, which was caused by a bacteria transmitted by the ever-present lice and fleas that tormented the men in the trenches.
83 Ruth's diary ends on this date. Interestingly, Clare Gass's diary has no entries from this date until Dec. 15, 1916.

Afterword

On October 25, 1968, the *Moncton Times* carried a brief obituary for "Miss R. Loggie." Ruth had died at home, the last surviving member of her family. The notice stated that she had had both local education and nurse training at Montreal General and had earned RN status before the war. It also informed the public that postwar, Ruth had returned to Canada and resumed "nursing in Montreal." Indeed, records reveal that in 1931, she shared the same Montreal address as her longtime friend Clare Gass.[1] It further revealed that Ruth had returned to her home at Burnt Church in 1938 "to care for members of her family who were ill." This would have included her younger brother Len who died in 1945. As for her friend Clare, extended family members recall her and her amputee brother Cyril visiting Ruth at Burnt Church over the course of many summers. One-legged Cyril left a lasting impressing by jumping off the wharf and swimming in the ocean.[2] Ruth's dear sister Rachael, the Ray/Rae of her diary, had also predeceased her, passing away in May of 1960.

The newspaper's death notice fell far short of doing Ruth justice. Unintentionally, it perpetuated a frequent slight to the Great War nurses of the CAMC. The obit characterized her four-year role in France as that of "a nursing assistant." This is not understatement but simply untrue. It is part of a tradition of underrating, underestimating, and even distorting the significant role of women like Ruth Loggie, Clare Gass, and all the other nurses of the CAMC during the Great War. Ruth was a graduate nurse and, as the diary makes abundantly clear, could manage very well in her ever evolving and most challenging duties.

Sadly, these challenges included more immediate matters than wounds and the enemy, for the nurses had to contend with the Victorian paternalism and outright double standard of the age. One clear example of this was the sinking of the *Lusitania* while they were at sea travelling to England. Dr Archibald of the McGill Unit wrote his wife that while the male officers were aware of the disaster on May 8, "we were warned not to tell the nurses for fear of alarming them too much."[3] The nurses on board soon learned of the disaster from other sources. Even ten years after the war ended, this concern as to how the "weaker sex" handled such news was perpetuated by the author of the McGill Unit's official history. The author, Fetherstonhaugh, paid tribute "to the manner in which news of the disaster was received, referring particularly to the demeanour of the sisters [who]...permitted no uneasiness to mark their bearing."[4] Hundreds of CAMC nurses, including Ruth, had shown throughout four years of war that rather than cower, nurses, like their male doctor counterparts, could nobly bear up under unrelenting work, horrendous casualties, bombings, and shell-fire. By war's end, nurses like Ruth's friend Christina Watling[5] had medals testifying to their grit and endurance. The long, impressive list of medals awarded to Canadian nurses—which includes 9 Military Medals for bravery under fire, 69 Royal Red Cross (First Class), 274 Royal Red Cross (Second Class), and 120 Mentions in Despatches[6]—bears witness to the nurses' strength and achievement under extraordinary circumstances.

NOTES

1 General Directory of the Overseas Nursing Sisters Association of Canada, as reproduced in Mann, War Diary of Clare Gass, 268.

2 Memories of Barb Wilson of Newcastle shared during visit on Sept. 7, 2018.

3 E. A. Archibald to his wife, May 10, 1915 (Osler Library, McGill University Archives).

4 Fetherstonhaugh, No. 3 CGH, 15.

5 Royal Red Cross (Second Class).

6 See canadiangreatwarproject.com/Regimental/AwardsNursingSister.asp.

Appendix

NORTH SHORE LEADER, OCTOBER 31, 1968

MISS RUTH LOGGIE

THE DEATH OF MISS RUTH LOGGIE OCCURRED AT HER home in Burnt Church on October 24. Born in Burnt Church, she was a daughter of the late Donald and Mary Jane (Anderson) Loggie. She was the last surviving member of her family. She graduated from Montreal General Hospital as a Reg. N. and was a nursing assistant in the First World War and served four years in France. On returning to Canada she resumed nursing in Montreal and retired in 1938 when she returned to Burnt Church to care for members of her family who were ill. A cousin, Miss Joyce Anderson, lived with her. The body rested at her home. The funeral was held Sunday and interment was in St. David's Cemetery, Burnt Church. The service at the residence was conducted by Rev. Charles Swan, United Church minister at Tabusintac and Burnt Church.

Select Bibliography

Butler, Janet. *Kitty's War.* Brisbane: University of Queensland Press, 2013.

Bruce, Constance. *Humour in Tragedy.* London: Skeffington, 1918.

Clint, Mabel B. *Our Bit: Memories of War Service by A Canadian Nursing Sister.* Montreal: Barwick, 1934.

Cowen, Ruth, ed. *A Nurse at the Front: The First World War Diaries of Sister Edith Appleton.* London: Simon & Schuster, 2012.

Daly, Nora E. *Memoirs of a World War I Nurse.* Bloomington, IA: iUniverse, 2011.

Dewar, Katherine. *Called to Serve: Georgina Pope, Canadian Military Nursing Heroine.* Charlottetown: Island Studies Press, 2018.

———. *Those Splendid Girls: The Heroic Service of Prince Edward Island Nurses in the Great War: 1914–1918.* Charlottetown: Island Studies Press, 2014.

Glassford, Sarah and Amy Shaw. *A Sisterhood of Suffering and Service: Women and Girls of Canada and Newfoundland during the First World War.* Vancouver: UBC Press, 2012.

Fetherstonhaugh, R. C. *No. 3 Canadian General Hospital (McGill) 1914–1919.* Montreal: Gazette Printing, 1928.

Hallett, Christine E. *Veiled Warriors: Allied Nurses of the First World War.* Oxford: Oxford University Press, 2014.

Harris, Kirsty. *More Than Bombs and Bandages: Australian Army Nurses at Work in World War I.* Newport, NSW: Big Sky Publishing, 2001.

Hebb, Ross. *In Their Own Words: Three Maritimers Experience the Great War.* Halifax: Nimbus Publishing, 2018.

Joined by a River: History of Burnt Church and New Jersey. Altona, MB: Friesens, 2010.

Luard, Kathleen. *Diary of a Nursing Sister on the Western Front: 1914–1915.* Milton Keyes, UK: Leonaur, 2011.

Macphail, Andrew. *Official History of the Canadian Forces in the Great War 1914–1919: The Medical Services.* Ottawa: Acland, 1925.

Mann, Susan. *Margaret Macdonald: Imperial Daughter.* Montreal: McGill-Queen's University Press, 2005.

———, ed. *The War Diary of Clare Gass: 1915–1919*. Montreal: McGill-Queen's University Press, 2000.

McEwen, Yvonne. *In The Company of Nurses: The History of the British Army Nursing Service in the Great War.* Edinburgh: Edinburg University Press, 2014.

McKenzie, Andrea. *War-Torn Exchanges: The Lives and Letters of Nursing Sisters Laura Holland and Mildred Forbes.* Vancouver: UBC Press, 2014.

Nicholson, G. W. L. *Canada's Nursing Sisters.* Toronto: Samuel Hakkert and Company, 1975.

Powell, Anne. *Women in the War Zone.* Stroud, UK: The History Press, 2009.

Quiney, Linda J. *This Small Army of Women: Canadian Volunteer Nurses and the First World War.* Vancouver: UBC Press, 2017.

Quinn, Shawna. *Agnes Warner and the Nursing Sisters of the Great War.* Fredericton, NB: Goose Lane Editions, 2010.

Scott, Eric, ed. *Nobody Ever Wins a War: The World War I Diaries of Ella Mae Bongard, R.N.* Toronto: Green Dragon Press, 1997.

Toman, Cynthia. *Sister Soldiers of the Great War: The Nurses of the Canadian Army Medical Corps.* Vancouver: UBC Press, 2016.

Wilkinson, Maude. *Four Score and Ten.* Brampton, ON: Margaret M. Armstrong, 2003.

Wilson-Simmie, Katharine. *Lights Out: The Memoir of Nursing Sister Kate Wilson, Canadian Army Medical Corps.* Ottawa: CEF Books, 2004.

About the Author

ALTHOUGH ORIGINALLY FROM Nova Scotia's South Shore, Ross Hebb is now a long-term resident of his adopted province of New Brunswick. A graduate of King's College and Dalhousie University, Dr. Hebb received his PhD from the University of Wales, Lampeter in 2002. Along with volumes on Maritime Church history, he has also written about the golden age of shipbuilding at St. Martins on the Bay of Fundy. In 2014 he edited the collection *Letters Home: Maritimers and the Great War, 1914–1918*, and 2018, *In Their Own Words: Three Maritimers Experience the Great War.* Dr. Hebb is married and lives in Fredericton, NB.

Other Books by Ross Hebb

In Their Own Words

ISBN 978-1-77108-670-7

Letters Home

ISBN 978-1-77108-203-7